NEWSPAPER FEATURE WRITING

Len Granato

UNSW
PRESS

in association with Deakin University Press

A UNSW Press book
published in association with Deakin University Press

Published by
University of New South Wales Press Ltd
University of New South Wales
UNSW Sydney NSW 2052
AUSTRALIA
www.unswpress.com.au

National Library of Australia
Cataloguing-in-Publication entry:

> Granato, Len, 1938– .
> Newspaper feature writing.
>
> Includes index.
> ISBN 0 86840 453 5.
>
> 1. Feature writing. I. Title.
>
> 808.06607

Printed by
Learning Services, Deakin University, Geelong VIC 3217, Australia

Biographical Notes

Len Granato was the Journalism Coordinator and Associate Professor of Journalism at the Queensland University of Technology until his early retirement at the end of 1996.

He worked as a journalist for four newspapers in the United States before joining United Press International. In eight years with UPI he held senior editorial positions, including several in the New York world headquarters.

Granato earned a PhD at Southern Illinois University and lectured at four US universities, including the University of Arkansas at Little Rock, where he served five years as Head of the Department of Journalism, before coming to the then-QIT in 1979.

In 1986 he took a Professional Development Leave from QIT and worked for six months as a senior journalist at the *Queensland Times* in Ipswich to gain experience in Australian journalism, to become acquainted with modern practices and to freshen his writing and reporting skills.

After being out of daily journalism for 17 years, Granato won a highly commended citation in the Walkley Awards for an eight-part feature series on Street Kids in the *Queensland Times*.

Upon his return to QIT, he wrote the first edition of *Newspaper Feature Writing*, drawing on his own feature writing experience in the US and Australia, theories he had developed as a professional feature writer and as an academic, and his critiques of his students' feature-writing efforts, which were pointers to common problems encountered by beginning feature writers.

Acknowledgments

I wish to thank the *Queensland Times* for generously allowing me to make liberal use of the Street Kid series in these pages.

Thanks also to the generations of journalism students at the Queensland Institute/ University of Technology who helped me learn how to teach feature writing by providing the raw materials for the development of my theories.

Special mention must be made of my late mentor, Professor Cliff Lawhorne, who got me started teaching feature writing, and of the late Deakin University Journalism Professor John Avieson, without whose help and encouragement this book might never have seen the light of day. Thanks also to the folks at Deakin University Press and my editor, Fran O'Sullivan-Smith, of Learning Resources Services.

For the new chapter on Computer-assisted Reporting, I am indebted to the many US-based experts who shared their knowledge with me on that fantastic Professional Development Leave in 1995 and to others whom I know only in the virtual communities we shared; specifically to Australian freelancers Elizabeth Walton and Kimberley Ivory and *Courier-Mail* columnist Jo Oliphant for their generosity in sharing through email exchanges with me their online experiences; and to Journalism lecturers Kerry Green of the University of Queensland and Stephen Quinn of Deakin University for looking over the early draft of the chapter.

And special thanks as always go to Barbara for more than 30 years of love, support and tolerance. This book is dedicated to her.

L. G.
1997

CONTENTS

Chapter 3 QUOTATIONS   35

Chapter 4 LEADS AND ENDINGS   49

Chapter 5 THE BODY   69

PREFACE

Since the first edition (1990) and the revised edition (1992) of *Newspaper Feature Writing* appeared, a set of reporting techniques is changing the way journalists work in the United States. These techniques are known collectively as Computer-assisted reporting (CAR) and they will become important in Australian journalism. The main aims of this 1997 revised edition of *Newspaper Feature Writing* are to maintain and enhance the systematic, practical approach to feature writing pioneered in the earlier editions and, with the addition of Chapter 7, to help lecturers integrate CAR into their courses and to give working journalists some instruction in CAR.

CAR refers to journalists using computers to gather, store, retrieve and analyse information to produce news and feature stories. Journalists get story ideas and information from Internet and other online sources such as libraries, CD-ROMs, newspaper and magazine archives and other full-text databases. They can create their own databases and analyse the data with spreadsheets and database managers instead of relying spin doctors to interpret them. They can enrich their stories by using email to locate and "interview" experts all over the world. General assignment reporters, roundspeople and feature writers all can tap into thousands of usegroups, newsgroups, bulletin boards and listservs where people with common interests meet in cyberspace to exchange ideas and discuss and debate issues.

I became aware of the increasing importance of CAR in 1994, when I began surfing the Internet and joined several professional and academic journalism discussion lists. In 1995, I spent 10 weeks in the US on Professional Development Leave from the Queensland University of Technology. My program was a week-long seminar in CAR at the Poynter Institute for Media Studies in St Petersburg, Florida, and fact-finding visits to a dozen Journalism schools to consult with experts on how to teach CAR. The trip confirmed my estimation of the extent to which CAR has changed US journalism and journalism education. As with most US trends, these are sure to find their way Down Under.

Many US journalism educators believe that long-form writing will be a feature of the newspapers and magazines of the future, and especially on the Internet, where the "news hole" is infinite. Without the space limitations of printing on paper, journalists can produce much longer stories for online publications on the World Wide Web and on CD-ROMs. As well, stories can be told in cyberspace in hypertext and multimedia form — using combinations of text, sound and video with links to related pieces containing sidebars, backgrounders, amplifications and notes for further research. This is already happening on the websites of some US commercial media organisations.

Journalism educators across the US told a similar tale of struggling to squeeze CAR techniques into their curriculum yet retaining the traditional reporting and writing techniques that will never go out of fashion. Most US Journalism schools pack CAR into an advanced reporting elective done by a few final-year students. I believe that this approach is short-sighted and disadvantages undergraduate students. Rather, Journalism schools should consider sprinkling CAR assignments in print and broadcast reporting subjects throughout their courses so that every journalism student can learn the techniques, not just a few.

Many QUT students and professional journalists I had never met before have told me they found this book helpful to them. I think they found it so because it's not based primarily on abstract theories. It contains theory, of course, because a theory is but a way of explaining practice. But the book is based on practice, on heading off problems that can creep into the work of feature writers. I believe the acquisition of CAR skills will help feature writers solve the major problem of being spoon-fed by spin doctors.

A word of caution: Don't get carried away by the technology. It's only a tool. Computer-assisted reporting will not replace the traditional reporting and writing techniques of journalism. Rather, CAR enhances them, it complements them, it supplements them, it takes reporting to higher levels. CAR enables journalists to report more meaningfully and in more depth and to write stories that are more compelling. Though CAR will make their work more meaningful and raise its quality, journalists will wear out as much or more shoe leather, will make as many or more telephone calls, will grill as many or more sources, and will pore over as many or more documents as before.

So Journalism lecturers will continue to teach their students how to observe, how to conduct interviews, how to cover court proceedings, how to do property searches, how to lay out newspaper and magazine pages, how to write news and feature stories. Lecturers will still need to nurture in their students the traditional skills and attributes of journalism — a grounding in the journalistic skills, the development of a healthy curiosity and a nose for news, a healthy scepticism that does not descend to cynicism, a sense of mission to serve the public interest, a sense of outrage at injustice, appreciation for the ethics of the profession and for the processes of democracy.

These traditional skills and attributes, according to Professor Gerald Grow of Florida A&M University, "depend upon unofficial, private, rarely named ones — 'metaskills' ". He lists Clarity, Compassion, Conscience, Conscientiousness, and a Balanced Life. By Clarity, Prof Grow means the ability to focus on a task with an open mind. By Compassion he means the ability to assuage the pain that comes from seeing too much too clearly. By Conscience he means a commitment to the truth and the defence of everyone's freedom of expression. By Conscientiousness he means striving for a life of doing, rather than reflection. And by a Balanced Life he means a life outside your work where you can turn off and renew yourself.

The inclusion of Professor Grow's list of metaskills would not have been possible without CAR. I learned about them on an Internet discussion list, and our entire correspondence in which I asked and received permission to include them in these pages was conducted through email.

INTRODUCTION

The modern newspaper was devised in the early 1830s, first in London, then in New York, when some enterprising proprietors changed their business philosophy and practice. Up to that time, proprietors had sold their newspapers by yearly subscription, in advance, to the affluent middle and upper classes. Typically, proprietors financed these elite newspapers by donations from political factions and by subscription. These newspapers were stodgy in style, for their writers produced long-winded literary and philosophical essays, political tracts and items detailing financial and commercial transactions.

By the 1830s, however, the Industrial Revolution had drawn a huge number of people from their farms to the cities to take up factory jobs. Newspaper proprietors were aware of this burgeoning working class, of course, but could not attract them as readers with their traditional product. Firstly, not many of them could read or write. Secondly, they could not afford to subscribe to a newspaper for a year in advance. And thirdly, few were interested in philosophical, political, commercial and financial matters.

But the Industrial Revolution eventually wrought great social changes. Members of the new working class became ambitious for their children and wanted them to live better lives than they did. Eventually, the workers used their numbers to win the vote. Then they elected governments that provided free education for their children. Literacy rates rose dramatically, and employers paid higher wages to literate employees.

Wishing to take advantage of the rising literacy rate, some astute newspaper proprietors sought ways to attract working-class families as readers. The first barrier was price. No worker could afford to lay out money for a year's subscription to an elite newspaper. To lower the price per copy, proprietors sold space to advertisers. Because revenue from advertising thus subsidised the cost of producing a newspaper, proprietors no longer had to insist on per-year subscriptions to raise revenue. After some experimentation, they learned they could sell newspapers by the copy at a low price. Young boys took these cheaper newspapers into the streets and hawked them for a penny a copy, which gave the name Penny Press to newspapers of this type.

Writing for the Masses

The second barrier was content. Most workers and their families had little interest in literature, philosophy, finance and commerce. So Penny Press journalists went out and found subjects that did interest them — crime, sex, scandal, entertainment and sport. Thus, Penny Press writers abandoned the stodgy essay of the elite press and instead wrote narratives that emphasised human interest. This new content, aimed at entertaining as well as informing, was wildly successful, and proprietors rewarded writers who could produce such copy. Some New York penny newspapers increased their circulations from a few thousand in the 1830s to more than a million by the end of the century.

Most newspapers today combine elements of the elite press and the Penny Press. They publish serious economic, political, financial and commercial news. And they also publish human-interest feature stories about crime, sex, scandal, entertainment and sport.

Features became increasingly important after radio came onto the media scene. As DeFleur and Ball-Rokeach point out, whenever a new mass medium appears, existing media must modify their functions.[1] Radio had ramifications for newspapers because radio could take its listeners to the scene of events as they unfolded and could provide frequent updates to the news. These abilities enabled radio to take over the newspaper's previous function of being first with spot news. Television came along and added pictures to the sound. Newspapers therefore had to modify their practices. If radio and television excelled at covering breaking news, newspapers had the space to analyse, to background and to entertain in their news coverage.

Editors constantly strive to strike a balance between giving their readers what they want (mainly soft news such as features, crime, sex, novelty, sport and entertainment) and giving their readers what the editors believe the readers must have to perform their sociopolitical responsibilities (mainly hard news such as political, social and economic analyses).

Pioneer communication researcher Wilbur Schramm categorised the aims of these two kinds of content as providing immediate and delayed rewards for readers.[2] He said that people read human interest stories for immediate enjoyment, such as savouring a sporting victory or sharing the triumph of a battler. And, he said, they plow through complex analyses of new taxes or new regulations because they know they'll need the information later.

FEATURE WRITING AND THE FUNCTIONS OF THE MEDIA

The news media perform five activities in Western-type societies such as Australia. These activities are surveillance of the environment — the news function; correlation of the parts of society in responding to the environment — the editorial function; transmission of the cultural and social heritage from one generation to the next — the education function; provision of relief from the cares of the day — the entertainment function; and support of the economic system — the advertising function.[3]

This book is concerned only with feature stories, which appear in each of the five functions. Feature stories generally fall into two categories — news features and human-interest features. Since each serves a different purpose, you approach them differently.

News features are intended primarily to inform, but they frequently also entertain because they utilise human-interest feature writing techniques. Ideas for news features may be found within such traditional hard-news values as conflict, timeliness, consequence, prominence and proximity. Examples are background stories about the new Ministers in the Premier's Cabinet, a counsellor's work at a rape crisis centre, a new product whose backers claim will help you lose weight, the most popular automobile models among car thieves, the opening of a new international hotel, the issues behind the latest overseas coup or the effects of the Government's new tax program on individuals and families. A news feature, then, investigates a problem, backgrounds a news event, or identifies or analyses a trend.

On the other hand, a human-interest feature story is a creative, sometimes subjective, article designed primarily to entertain and only secondarily to inform. The assumption of the entertainment function is that readers need a breather from the stresses and strains of their daily lives and from the doom-and-gloom of much of the news. Newspapers provide such breathers — comic strips, games, puzzles, competitions and feature stories.

The feature stories of this type fall within the soft-news values of novelty and human interest. What distinguishes the human-interest story, then, is an emphasis on the human elements of the story rather than on its intrinsic importance. Such stories are worth doing because they appeal to people more or less naturally, not because they have any particular significance or importance. So they are anchored in the human emotions — joy, tragedy, humour, love, hate, sorrow, jealousy. They are written about the smaller accomplishments, insignificant human foibles and serendipitous happenings. Examples are stories about the nude wedding party, the man who collects farm tractors, the nuisance pigeons and the statue of the king, the 100th birthday, the 50th wedding anniversary, the singing dog, the man who repairs dolls, the house made entirely of bottles, the potion to remove warts, the personality profile of someone who is not well known.

As noted, such stories have little intrinsic news value, but they help balance the newspaper package of the day. Readers identify with other people, so they like stories about other people's successes and failures. Thus, human-interest features get a good run in any issue of a newspaper. So a working journalist or a free-lancer who can write sparkling, informative feature stories — both news features and human-interest features — will impress chiefs of staff and editors. Feature stories that sparkle are more complex than straight news stories because they require more research, what journalists call reporting. Once you have completed the reporting for a feature story, you have at your disposal a number of proven writing techniques that will make your stories sparkle, that will bring the people in them to life.

THE TECHNIQUES OF FEATURE WRITING

This book will teach you how to think like a feature writer and how and when to use these techniques. If you have had experience in newswriting and reporting, so much the better, but even if you have not, this book can help you report and write well, perhaps well enough to sell stories to newspapers and magazines. In writing this book, I have used the very techniques that the book itself suggests that you use when you write feature stories. The writing is bright and breezy, almost conversational, and I have provided practical examples of the writing theories I espouse. Some of these theories may be familiar to you, but most I have developed myself from more than 40 years of journalistic writing and more than 25 years of teaching university students how journalists write. Up to now, my theories have been available only to my students. This book now makes them available to working journalists and to the general public.

Chapter 1, Getting Started, shows you how feature writing differs from other kinds of journalistic writing in approach and technique. As well, you will find hints about how to think up ideas for feature stories and how to focus your general ideas to the narrow, specific, manageable size necessary for execution.

In **Chapter 2, Reporting**, you will learn how to gather information for your feature stories. The chapter contains such topics as strategies to use in your interviews, the use of body language, how to ask questions, what kinds of questions to ask, when to use and when not to use a tape recorder and how to deal with sources who ask for anonymity.

Since good quotations are your most powerful feature writing tool, all of **Chapter 3, Quotations**, is devoted to handling them. You will learn how to select quotations for inclusion, how to prune rambling quotations, how to foreshadow quotations so your story keeps moving forward, how to create the illusion that the reader is present as your sources speak in your feature story.

Once you have completed the reporting, you begin to write your feature story. In **Chapter 4, Leads and Endings**, you will learn how answering the feature frame question helps you set your final focus, how to organise your material and how to use suspended interest. You will encounter several ways of beginning a story. Because ending a feature story well is as important as starting it well, this chapter also shows you how to write endings.

In **Chapter 5, The Body**, you learn about the part of the story between the first paragraph and the last paragraph. You will discover such techniques as creating peaks and valleys, telling anecdotes like jokes, taking the reader to the scene with good description, using the second-person plural, spiraling your writing, blocking your paragraphs and backgrounding your subjects.

Chapter 6, Putting it all Together, features the paragraph-by-paragraph analysis of a full-length feature story from the Street Kids series. The commentary shows you the techniques in action and how failure to use a technique can bog down a story.

And **Chapter 7, Computer-assisted Reporting**, introduces you to a new set of reporting techniques that eventually will revolutionise journalism in Australia. You will learn how to use email to find story ideas and to interview sources wherever they live in the world and how spreadsheets and databases can help free you from the influence of spin doctors.

To paraphrase the lead character in the motion picture *All that Jazz* who was talking about dancing, this book can't make you a great writer and maybe it can't even make you a good writer. But if you follow its suggestions and work hard, it will make you a better writer.

---

[1] DeFleur, M. L., and Ball-Rokeach, S. J. (1989) *Theories of mass communication.* 5th ed. New York: Longman.

[2] Schramm, W. (1949). The nature of news. *Journalism Quarterly.* 26, p. 259–269.

[3] Wright, C. R. (1986). *Mass communication: A sociological perspective.* 3rd ed. New York: Random House.

Chapter 1
GETTING STARTED

Feature writers provide creative insights within the realm of facts. Facts are important. It's important to keep in mind that as journalists, feature writers are confined by the facts as they find them. Feature writers may not falsify or otherwise enhance facts for the sake of a story. They must never tamper with the facts, either by acts of commission or by acts of omission. Misrepresenting the facts is as great a journalistic sin as falsifying them.

However, feature writers are allowed more creativity than news writers in treating the facts. Feature writers operate outside the confines of who, what, where, when, why and how — the 5 Ws and the H that define the limits of newswriting. They do this through such devices as using informal or dramatic language and style, addressing the reader directly by use of the second person plural "you", delving deeply into the "why" and the "how" of a story, providing colour and description and writing about feelings.

Feature writers provide humanistic understandings and human involvements, give us small glimpses of human foibles, note the transitory and the unessential and go beyond the facts to describe colour and feelings. Thus, all feature writing is dramatic writing. Features are written according to the tone and mood of the content. A feature story is therefore more subjective than a straight-news story.

But your feature story cannot become too subjective, for unless your assignment is specifically to be a commentator, no newspaper will allow you to use its columns to foist your opinions on its readers. In fact, it is unethical for you as a journalistic writer to try to use a newspaper that way. So if you are not a commentator, the subjectivity in your feature stories should come in your descriptions and in your interpretation of facts, not in your straight-out opinions about how things ought to be. Remember always that you are striving for creativity within the realm of facts. Still, feature writing does afford you immense scope to show off your individuality in approach, style and writing. But before you get into the details of how to exploit this larger scope, you need a conceptual overview of the entire feature-writing process.

THE PROCESS IN A NUTSHELL

The starting point for writing a feature story is thinking up an idea for a subject to write about. The traditional news values are helpful because as a journalist you are always looking for subjects that embody one or several of these values.

In feature writing your options for stories are almost endless. You can work within the hard news values and write a news feature or a human-interest feature involving conflict, timeliness, proximity or prominence. Or you can work within the soft news values of novelty and human interest and write a feature story about somebody or something interesting but not intrinsically important. Once you have decided upon a suitable general subject, you must narrow it to a manageable size. This is called setting the focus, which at this point is a tentative idea of what your story will be about. It is important that you set a focus because you could research and write any number of stories on your general subject. So you must have some idea early in the process of which story you are going to do.

Once you have a tentative idea of what your story will be about, you gather information about your subject by observing, interviewing and reading. Journalists call these activities "reporting". After you have observed the scene, conducted interviews and read documents, you should have a much clearer idea of the direction your story should take. You might even abandon your proposed focus on the basis of what you have learned and do an entirely different story. More likely, though, you will probably find that you must further narrow your subject and refine your focus so that it more precisely delineates the direction of the story.

Then you organise your material in such a way that you retain for possible inclusion information that fits the focus and eliminate information that does not. You might fine-tune your focus so that it encompasses particularly good information that you don't want to eliminate. In this planning stage, you should be ruthless in selecting what to include and what to eliminate as you narrow your subject further and give it direction, theme and focus. Then you write and rewrite your story, using a variety of techniques.

COMING UP WITH IDEAS

Good feature writing starts with a good idea. Unless an editor or a chief of staff assigns a specific story to you, you'll have to think up your own ideas, and writers who can regularly do that are highly prized on newspaper staffs. If you're a free-lancer, you not only have to think up your own ideas, but you also have to persuade newspaper and magazine editors that these stories are worth doing, that you are competent to do them and that they should pay you for doing them.

Where do ideas come from? They are all around you, readily at hand and in cyberspace. You find ideas by watching, reading, listening and by tuning in on what's happening in your street, your suburb, your community, your city, the state, the nation, the world and outer space. Talk regularly to people who are not journalists. They will mention things that interest them, and might inspire you to write stories on some of those topics. Another good way to come up with story ideas is to read widely. You should regularly read a variety of Australian metropolitan, regional, provincial and suburban newspapers and magazines aimed at various target audiences. The Internet makes hundreds of overseas newspapers and magazines available to you. Many have online editions, and commercial online providers maintain full-text, searchable databases of hundreds more magazine and newspapers. You could do a local version of a story done in *The Times* of London or the *Rocky Mountain News* or the *Toronto Globe and Mail* or *USAToday*. As well, listen to local and national talk-back radio and current affairs programs and watch current affairs television programs. The point of all this reading, listening and viewing is to keep up with current issues, to know what people are talking about and to see what other journalists have written about.

You must take this tack because journalists don't just write about topics that interest them as individuals. Rather, they write about topics that might interest a public audience, they write for anyone out there who might happen to start reading a publication in which their story appears. In other words, a journalist's perception of audience wants and needs is a major factor in deciding what to write about. Never assume that your audience shares your interests. It is up to you to determine and cater for the interests of your audience.

The traditional news values aid you in selecting subjects likely to interest your audience. The necessity of identifying audience interests requires journalists to tune into their community by reading, listening and watching. And to protect yourself against becoming jaded and inward looking in your perceptions of what's important in the outside world, take part in nonjournalistic activities to put yourself in contact with a wide variety of people who can give you ideas for stories, whether or not they know they are doing so.

A PERSONAL EXPERIENCE

You cannot predict how and when an idea will occur to you, and frequently one idea leads to others. Consider my own experience in 1986. I was on leave from the Queensland Institute of Technology in Brisbane to work for six months as a journalist at the *Queensland Times*. My rental house in Ipswich was a five-minute drive from the *Queensland Times*, and for those five minutes every morning I listened to a Brisbane talk-back radio program conducted by Haydn Sargent.

One morning a young man telephoned and complained to Sargent that he and his mates had been talking in an Ipswich public park late the previous night and the police had run them off for no good reason. When I arrived at the *Queensland Times*, I suggested to the editor and the chief of staff that I seek permission to ride with police officers in patrol cars on the overnight shift to write feature stories on what went on while most of Ipswich was asleep. The police gave permission for me to ride three nights, and I eventually wrote a five-part feature series, which made the original story idea a great success.

But beyond that, riding with the police that first night led me to another, better, more poignant feature series. The policemen I was riding with assisted in the arrest of two street kids. One was arrested near a double-decker bus from which a group of adults handed out coffee, tea and biscuits. A social worker came to the watchhouse after midnight to help the kids who'd been arrested.

All of this aroused my curiosity. Who were these kids? Why were they on the street? How many kids live on the street in Ipswich? Why? Who were those adults dispensing refreshments from the double-decker bus? What were they trying to accomplish? What about that social worker who got out of bed to help?

Here was a second story idea developing out of the first idea. A little preliminary research revealed that the adults at the bus were members of a born-again fundamentalist Christian church who had taken on as a ministry the rehabilitation of Ipswich street kids. A few telephone calls to social welfare agencies turned up the fact that scores of Ipswich kids were living on the streets for one reason or another. Several news values were obviously present: conflict, children, religion, proximity, timeliness, crime, human interest. Here was a story worth doing.

The street kid story took on a life of its own and ultimately became an eight-part feature series that was highly commended in the 1986 Walkley Awards. So because I didn't waste that five-minute drive to the office but instead tuned in to a talk-back radio program, I got a story idea that developed into a five-part feature series on police work and an eight-part feature series on street kids that won national recognition. A total of 13 feature stories and a national award sprang from that five-minute scrap of Haydn Sargent's program. You just never know where an idea's going to come from, so you have to be constantly on the alert.

Some useful hints about coming up with ideas

Because employers value journalists who can think up their own ideas, I have always required my tertiary students to come up with their own ideas, within categories that I provide. Usually, the categories I give them are an inanimate object, a personality profile of a non-celebrity and a person with an unusual job. I pick those categories for educational reasons, but there are many other kinds of feature stories, of course. Some other types are how-to stories in which you explain a process, a backgrounder to an issue or a person in the news, a case history of a problem or a solution, a story about a person with an unusual hobby or collection, a first-person account of an experience, an anniversary story, a seasonal story (Christmas, Anzac Day).

Over the years my students have written feature stories on hundreds of topics. Here are just a few: the effects of computerisation on automobile maintenance, case studies of Filipinas who married Australian men, use of performance-enhancing drugs by athletes and sportsmen, the competition among major brewers, problems in IVF programs, tobacco advertising and teenagers, increasing use of condoms in the wake of AIDS, a specialised cinema that screens films shunned by the big houses, the history of the toothbrush and of the wedding ring, a singing Council bus driver, a local leading fashion designer, prominent State and Local politicians, what it's like to ride a new roller coaster, a tourist attraction house made entirely of bottles, buskers in the city mall, a restaurant with a resident ghost, the Phantom fan club, historic buildings, activists of all stripes, tarot card readers, prostitutes and strip-tease artists of both sexes, reformed drug addicts and alcoholics, mortuary workers, guinea pig breeders, possum hunters, the City Council's rat-catching terriers, the local gossip, various local sportspeople, a new shopping centre, the doll hospital.

How to focus in on an idea

Many students panic when they are told at the first meeting of the feature writing class that they must bring a story idea to the second meeting a week later. They panic because they don't think they can do it. But that's only because they've never had to do it before. They *can* do it. They *do* do it. They do it because they have to do it. We give them a little preparation, of course. It goes something like this.

The quest for a subject to write about begins with thinking in broad concepts and ends with a narrow single, manageable concept as you refine your thinking. Suppose, in casting around for something to write about, you decide that the news value "animals" will give you a nice change of pace from the kinds of stories you've been writing lately. Obviously, you can't write a meaningful and interesting 1,000 word feature story on animals. You have to narrow your topic to manageable size.

So what animal are you going to write about? Whales? Snails? Elephants? Kittens? Feral cats? Tigers? Moths? Mosquitoes? Butterflies? Dogs? Cows? Prize bullocks? Horses? Sheep? Bats?

You decide to write a feature story about dogs. Why do you decide on dogs? Who can tell? Sometimes it's difficult to say why or how a writer comes to this kind of decision. Sometimes you know why you select a category, sometimes you don't. Maybe you like dogs, maybe you hate dogs, maybe you have absolutely no position on dogs. Maybe you have dogs in the back of your mind because you read a story in a magazine about them or because one woke you up with its barking in the middle of the night or because your daughter wants one for Christmas or because one knocked over your garbage can last week or because you saw an RSPCA warden pick up a stray. Follow your impulse, even if you don't know where it comes from. For whatever reason, you have decided on a dog story.

Now what kind of dogs? Labradors? Dingoes? German shepherds? Collies? Pig dogs? Corgies? Big dogs? Little dogs? Common dogs? Rare dogs? Working dogs? Pet dogs? Expensive dogs? Inexpensive dogs? Pedigreed dogs? Mutts? Wild dogs? Abandoned dogs? Neighbourhood nuisance dogs? Stray dogs? Dogs used in medical research?

You decide to write a feature story about working dogs.

Now what kind of working dogs? Guard dogs at military installations? Junk yard dogs? Police dogs? Drug-sniffer dogs? Cattle dogs? Sheep dogs? Guide dogs? Dogs that act in movies and television commercials? Circus dogs?

You decide to write a feature story about guide dogs.

Now what kind of story about guide dogs? How they are selected? How they are trained? Personality spotlight of a trainer? Case studies of blind people and their dogs? The problems faced by authorities and blind people because of the shortage of suitable dogs? How dogs came to play their role as eyes for blind people? Which breeds of dogs are most and least suitable? The anguish caused to blind people through the loss of their dogs? Heartwarming stories of the love between owners and their dogs?

You decide to write a feature story about the problems faced by authorities and blind people because of the shortage of suitable dogs.

Once you reach this point, you are ready to think about how you will go about getting the information you require for the story. Obviously, a story about the problems caused by a shortage of dogs suitable for training to work with blind people will send you to different sources of information than a story about drug-sniffing dogs or the dogs that ride the ponies in the circus. Once you have pinpointed your proposed focus, you are ready to start your reporting.

You should go through a similar process each time you face the task of thinking up a story idea for a feature story. The more planning you can put into it at the beginning, the easier your task will be. Your proposed focus is your blueprint. It points you in the direction you must go for your information. As well, it points you away from unfruitful directions. In other words, the thinking time you put in at this stage saves you legwork time later. So that when you begin your reporting activities, you head straight for the highest and best sources of information for the specific story you have in mind.

Chapter 2
REPORTING

Journalists can report in only three ways — by observing events directly, by reading documents and by interviewing people. You observe by being there and by paying close attention. Some sources will give you documents, but you will consult other documents yourself before going to interviews. The obvious documents in this category are biographical dictionaries and newspaper clips about your subject. Many working and freelance journalists keep large clip files of topics they think they might write about someday and have access to newspaper libraries or online databases. If you have a home computer and a modem, it would be a good idea to subscribe to an online provider that offers access to newspaper and magazine databases. Such a service is invaluable, both for generating story ideas and for doing background research.

Whether you are observing, reading or interviewing, successful reporting will depend on good notetaking. This is true even if you interview with a tape recorder. Taking good notes is important for accuracy's sake. It's best if you use a shorthand system, such as Teeline, but if you can't, then develop your own system. The Australian Journalists' Association section of the Media, Entertainment and Arts Alliance industrial awards recognise the importance of increasing proficiency in shorthand.

DEALING WITH SOURCES: BIAS, FAIRNESS AND BALANCE

When you observe something yourself, you can report it on your own authority. In other words, you are the source of that information. Information obtained from documents or interviews, however, must be attributed to an outside source. Attribution validates the information and allows your reader to evaluate it. Readers normally are entitled to know where all the information in your story came from.

After all, it makes a difference whether a statement about the Budget comes from the Treasurer, or from the Leader of the Opposition, from your butcher or from you. Journalists try to get information from the highest and best source available in the interests of validity and believability.

One fact of life that journalists have to live with and compensate for is that every source is motivated by bias and tries to influence them. Sources are biased because they have a vested interest in what information about them is reported and how that information is reported. There is nothing wrong or suspicious about this. Everyone in a democratic society has a right to identify problems, to advocate solutions, and to try to persuade the public to adopt his or her policies instead of someone else's. One way sources try to persuade the public is by getting their views into newspaper and radio and television stories by talking to journalists or by giving them documents.

When dealing with a journalist, a source presents his or her case in the best possible light. Since you can't expect anyone to point out the weaknesses and fallacies in his or her own arguments, the journalist draws out as much information from the source as possible, then seeks contrary views from people with different biases who oppose that source's point of view. This is how a journalist achieves fairness and balance in his or her stories.

So while it is perfectly proper for sources to be biased, a journalist must not be biased. While sources reveal or conceal information according to their advantage, journalists must never do this when performing professional duties. It is unethical to do this. You should not accept or reject or use or not use information on the basis of your personal or political preferences, but on the basis of its value to your story. You take information as it comes to you and strive to produce a fair and balanced article by talking to people with different views. For example, a journalist balances highly favourable comments about the Budget from the Treasurer with highly unfavourable comments from the Shadow Treasurer.

DOCUMENTS: THEIR USES AND PITFALLS

When a journalist asks for information, most experienced sources are helpful most of the time because they want to get their point of view across and they know that the opposing point of view will be in the journalist's story. So in addition to granting interviews, many sources often give you such documents as biographies, press releases, texts of speeches and reports to assist you in putting their views across, but also to try to influence you. Such documents save you time by freeing you from having to ask about purely background matters and from going over old ground. You can therefore concentrate in interviews on discovering and exploring new information or new aspects of old information.

Another important thing to know about documents is that sources often leak them to journalists. Because all sources have vested interests, they leak documents for reasons of their own — whether altruistic or self-serving. Someone who wants to see justice done might leak a document to a journalist in the hope of setting things right through the power of the press. Another might leak a document for reasons of personal revenge or partisan gain. Someone else might leak a document to test public reaction. If public reaction is negative, the person responsible can say the document was only one option among many being considered and let it die a natural death. But if public reaction is favourable, the person responsible can come forward and claim the credit for the policy.

Likewise, someone opposed might leak the document to you hoping to scuttle a planned policy through premature disclosure. Such leaks often come from politicians from both sides who disagree with the Leader but don't want to lose their jobs. Sources offer almost all leaked documents with the proviso that the journalist not reveal the name of the person who supplied the document. If you promise confidentiality to a source, you are bound by the AJA Code of Ethics not to reveal his or her identity.

THE INTERVIEW: THE BASIC JOURNALISTIC TOOL

Since journalists can't always be present and documents don't always have all the information a journalist needs, interviews provide the basis for most stories. You will discover early in the game that every interview is different. There are no formalised procedures that will work every time, in every interview. Common sense and experience dictate what you will do and how you will act, for an interview is not just asking questions and writing down answers. It is a complex social interaction, a dynamic human relationship, a delicate give-and-take between two people, an exercise in role-playing, a fragile journalistic tool. In an interview, a source tries to put his or her views in the best possible light and the journalist tries to worm as much pertinent information out of that source as possible. One of the factors that complicates the interview situation is that many times the source is seeking consensus for his or her position while the journalist is looking for conflict between that source and other sources.[1]

Sometimes people are reluctant to grant interviews to journalists for reasons they consider sufficient — maybe they've never been interviewed before and are afraid they'll be treated like some people they've seen interviewed on television by callous, confrontational and rude journalists; maybe they have something to hide; maybe they can't spare the time to see you; or maybe they don't see the journalistic value in what they say or do. Your job is to get the story, so you must make every effort to persuade them to grant you an interview. There are some ploys you can use in trying to persuade them.

- You can try flattery: "Joe Bloggs suggested I talk to you because you have a good grasp of the situation."

- You can appeal to the person to help you: "I've almost got everything I need for this story but I really need a comment or two from you to make it complete."

- You can indicate that you're off on a wrong tangent to tempt the person to correct your information: "We've got this tip that's probably not true [it isn't] but we need a comment from you explaining it."

- Or, as a last resort only, you can get tough: "We're running this story anyway, with or without your comments. I'm going to write that you were offered a chance to comment and that you declined, and people may wonder why you didn't want to talk about it. You're going to make yourself look bad if you don't comment on this."

PLAY EACH INTERVIEW BY EAR

Take each interview as it comes and play it by ear. Some sources find it difficult to talk and some will talk forever if you let them. Some like to chit-chat, some need to brag about themselves, some want to get right down to the business at hand. You should humour your sources. With a reticent source, don't interrupt but keep the questions coming. Don't let the interview falter or you'll have to prime your source every time he or she hesitates. But let a garrulous source set the pace. You've got that source talking, so keep quiet yourself. Chime in with questions to get more detail, or to get back on track or to change subjects. And expect the garrulous source you interviewed yesterday to turn reticent today, or vice versa. After all, people change from day to day. They have moods, they're more interested in talking about some things than about others and they have more time on some days than on others.

There are many kinds of journalistic interviews. Some are conducted on the run under great deadline pressure, some are conducted by telephone. But we are interested in interviewing for feature stories. Usually, this means in-depth, in-person interviews. You need time to probe. Your job is to capture the person on paper, using direct and indirect quotations, descriptions of personality, physical characteristics and surroundings and anecdotes, anecdotes and anecdotes. So you must be constantly alert for angles. You need time for that, and you need to be there to do that. The telephone will not do for this kind of interview.

While the interview is in progress, you must keep in mind which bits you'll definitely use, which you might use and which you probably won't use. But you have to stay alert because you always have to be ready to shift any piece of information from one category to another in your mind. To be able to do this, you should constantly be comparing every new piece of information with everything else you've heard.

PLAN, PLAN, PLAN

Obviously, complex interviews that lead to in-depth stories require careful planning beforehand. The first step is to define who you need to interview to get the story you're looking for. This means that during the idea stage you figure out what story you want and who can give you the information you need. You want the highest and best source available. Know exactly who your main subject has to be and figure out what kind of third parties you'll need to talk to. Often the main subject can suggest specific third parties.

Then background the main subject and the topic in general. Look up well-known main subjects in dictionaries of biography. Check clip files or databases for previous stories about the person and the general topic so you won't waste time asking about things that are already on the record. The background you unearth will also be helpful as a springboard for your questions.

When you telephone to request an appointment for an interview, tell the interviewee briefly about your focus and indicate how much time you'll need for the interview. After all, you are asking a busy person to spare you valuable time to help you with a project of yours. Be as specific as you can about the story you are doing so the interviewee can prepare for the interview. Journalists are bound by the AJA Code of Ethics to identify themselves and an employer, if any, before obtaining an interview for publication. People are entitled to know when they are talking to a journalist for publication.

TELEPHONES AND TAPE RECORDERS

For feature stories and other in-depth pieces, you must interview your main sources in person for best results. Telephone calls may do for news interviews, where speed is important and all you need are quick answers to straight-forward questions. But for feature stories you need colour and description and, above all, time to encourage a source to open up to you. So you simply must interview in person. Another disadvantage of telephone interviewing is the loss of visual feedback, so you cannot check body language. As if these disadvantages were not enough, being interviewed by telephone can intimidate sources who are not accustomed to talking for publication. And since you can't see your source's reactions, you may be unaware of the intimidation and therefore don't know you have a problem.

Another modern device that can intimidate some sources is the tape recorder. Tape recorders help accuracy because you get every word. But they are dreadfully slow because it takes exactly as much time to listen to the tape as it did to conduct the interview. Of course, tape recorders do not intimidate sources accustomed to journalistic interviews. Indeed, some of them have even taken to using their own recorders to protect themselves against being misquoted or misinterpreted by the journalists who interview them.

But a person who is not accustomed to being interviewed might freeze up when you bring out the tape recorder. So if you use a tape recorder with such a source, use a small one with a built-in microphone, and let him or her become accustomed to its presence before you start the interview proper. Just place it unobtrusively between you and turn it on while you're still at the small-talk stage, being careful that it's not near an appliance whose electromagnetic field can "jam" your taping. Before long, the recorder blends into the surroundings and you can proceed with your questions.

Before you go to the interview, check your recorder. If it's battery-operated, make sure the batteries are fresh and that you have spare batteries with you as well. Before you begin the interview, check it again to make sure it's still working. Most journalists can tell you horror stories about returning from an interview and finding that the recorder that worked perfectly at home failed at the source's office for one reason or another. So even if you use a tape recorder, take some notes during the interview to protect yourself against a breakdown. Use a recorder that has a digital counter so you can note the location of quotes to find them quickly later.

It's a good idea to transcribe your interviews. Unfortunately, it takes three to four hours to transcribe one hour of tape, so working journalists rarely have the luxury of being able to transcribe. If you can take the time, by all means do so. The very act of transcribing takes you slowly and thoroughly over the interview again, this time looking for a focus and consciously evaluating information for inclusion. And sometimes you get double duty from the information — when you can use material gathered for one story in some other story. If you have pertinent direct quotations already available in a computer file, you can save yourself a lot of legwork.

THOSE CRITICAL FIRST FEW MINUTES

Arrive at the interview on time. The first few minutes of an interview are critical. They can make you or break you, because first impressions play an important part in interpersonal relations. So it's important to make a good first impression on your source. Dress appropriately for the occasion. In other words, don't wear a sloppy joe and jeans to interview a businessperson and don't dress up to interview street kids. And speak appropriately, because your source is more likely to trust your ability to write the language correctly if you speak it correctly.

Some people say that you should try to make sources like you. Others, however, say that it's not important for them to like you. It's enough that they understand you and respect you as a professional. Your attitude should be professional. You should be an equal to those you interview. Feel sure of yourself. Be direct and confident. Don't be overawed by people in high places, and never talk up or down to people. When you meet a source, instantly gauge the best way to present yourself based on your first impressions of that person at that time in that setting. The more interviews you conduct, the more confidence you will have in your ability to assess sources accurately.

In any case, be careful not to overdo the establishment of rapport because you run the risk of receiving socially acceptable answers instead of the truth. But social convention usually demands a bit of small talk to break the ice before getting down to the business at hand. Keep your conversation openers neutral. Greet the source by using his or her name correctly. This is a subtle way of conveying professional competence from the first statement you make. You might comment about a personal effect in the surroundings, such as the picture of the spouse on the desk or the award hanging on the wall. If you have mutual acquaintances, mention them. If you know from your background reading the person's interests, hobby or sport, comment knowingly on it. As a last resort you can comment on the weather or refer to a current event. But if you make a comment about a political current event, be sure your comment is nonpartisan so you don't risk starting off by saying something the source disagrees with.

You and Your Sources

For your part, you need not like or approve of your source to do a good job as a journalist. Your primary responsibility is to your reader, not to your source. Under the AJA Code of Ethics, journalists "shall report and interpret the news with scrupulous honesty by striving to disclose all essential facts and by not suppressing relevant, available facts or distorting by wrong or improper emphasis." That's what you owe your reader. All you owe your source is to report fairly and accurately what he or she says and does and to respect confidentiality if you have given your word to do so.

One of the facts of journalistic life is that you sometimes have to associate publicly and professionally with people — sources — you would not want to be seen with privately. As a professional, however, you must be prepared to interview anyone, and you must treat every source with courtesy, dignity and respect. This means every source, the ones you despise as well as the ones you admire. Don't let your negative feelings about a source influence your interviews. Your facial expressions and tone of voice can broadcast your dislike or disapproval. So be aware of your biases and work on reducing their influence on your mannerisms, on your tone of voice and on how you word your questions. Be sincerely interested in your source and what your source is telling you, and always phrase your questions calmly, clearly and matter-of-factly.

Choreographing the Setting

When you sit down for an interview, try to choreograph the setting, though this may be difficult on the source's turf. You want a clear line of sight so that you can establish and maintain eye contact, but your source should not be able to read your notes. Try to avoid sitting on opposite sides of a desk or table, because such a seating arrangement is confrontational and best used for serious negotiation. Ideally, to achieve an arrangement that encourages cooperation, you and the source should be sitting in chairs at slight angles to one another with your chair pointed toward the source's. Or, alternatively, sit on the same side of a desk or table and turn toward the source, or sit at right angles at a desk or table. Maintain as much eye contact as you can. Although it's difficult to look your source in the eye and write at the same time, you have to do both.

Be aware of the distance between you and your source and try to vary the distance according to your needs of the moment.[2] In our society, the intimate distance between two people is less than 45 centimetres, or about 18 inches. Personal distance extends from about 45 centimetres to about 1.2 metres, or about 4 feet. And social distance extends from about 1.2 metres to 4 metres, or about 13 feet. You can put this knowledge to good use during interviews by altering the distance between you and your source. Of course, this is not always possible, but the idea is to place yourself at the appropriate distance for the nature of the question you are asking at that time.

It would usually be socially and culturally inappropriate for you to be closer than 45 centimetres when you interview someone, so try to be just within the personal zone, about 55 to 60 centimetres, or about 2 feet, away from your source. Be subtle about it, but lean forward when you ask a question that is significantly more personal than the ones you have been asking. By leaning forward, you intrude into the intimate zone. Your intrusion should be non-threatening and encouraging because you hope to unconsciously induce your source to take you into his or her confidence. Then, for a less personal question, you lean back to vacate the intimate zone and return to the personal zone. This restores the social situation to its previous state and may give your source a vague sense of relief that you can jar later with another personal question.

A much stronger use of body language would be a move toward the source that brought you well within the intimate zone. This would be more than an intrusion into the zone; it would be an invasion. A step forward is therefore confrontational and is meant to convey to the source that you expect an honest answer to a tough question — or else. This confrontational tactic might be useful on some news features or investigative features where sources might be evasive or hostile but would almost never be appropriate during an interview for a human-interest feature.

BASIC STRATEGIES IN QUESTIONING AND NOTE-TAKING

It's a good idea to write some questions down in advance and take them to the interview. It doesn't happen often, but occasionally you stumble onto a blockbuster while doing a routine story. If you need a moment to collect your thoughts because the source just said something that flabbergasted you, being able to glance down at a question written beforehand can be a lifesaver and keep the interview flowing. Prepared questions can also bail you out if you suddenly dry up during a line of questioning. You just switch to a question on your prepared list and go on from there.

In your questioning, don't forget journalistic basics. Ask about the 5 Ws and the H. You won't have a story if you neglect one of those. And "how" and "why" questions are particularly good for eliciting more information because they are open-ended and permit the source to answer with relative freedom. Asking open-ended questions encourages a source to open up topic areas that you might not have considered. Open-ended questions are helpful in getting a source to expand and can act as a safety valve by allowing a source to let off steam about a bothersome topic. Disadvantages to open-ended questions are that they tend to be incomplete because they permit the source to take any direction and the journalist may have trouble determining where the source stands on an issue. On the other hand, closed questions — those in which you have specified options, such as yes/no or favour/oppose — restrict the scope of the answers and force your source to take a position.

In your interviews, use closed and open-ended questions for different purposes. You can begin with open-ended questions to let the source reveal general thoughts and explore the issues, then switch to closed questions to pin down specific positions. Or you can begin with closed questions to establish specific positions, then follow up with open-ended questions to give the source a chance to elaborate. Or you can mix closed and open-ended questions within topics.

Take notes on your source's comments, on description, on atmosphere, and on your impressions. Hold your notebook so that your source cannot see the page. You will not always be writing down what the source is saying, and if the source can see the page, he or she might get miffed if you are writing down something else or if you have stopped writing altogether. A miffed source might clam up for the rest of the interview. So keep moving your pencil, even if you are doodling through a boring patch. As long as your pencil is moving, your source is likely to keep talking.

THE IMPORTANCE OF ANECDOTES AND THIRD PARTIES

What you are constantly listening for are good direct quotations, particularly in the telling of a good anecdote, because anecdotes are the heart and soul of the feature story. Anecdotes can be humourous or serious, happy or sad, positive or negative. They illuminate your subject's personality and show the ways he or she does things.

They demonstrate his or her attitudes and outlooks. They document significant occasions and influences in his or her life. They provide incidents that illustrate some point you are making about the source. Because of all these contributions, anecdotes play the major role in personalising your story. You gather anecdotes from your main source and from third parties by asking questions. Because you are not seeking to pin down specific positions but are looking for stories, you should ask open-ended questions that give the source as wide a scope as possible. Examples of such questions might be:

- What's the most interesting (humourous, satisfying, mystifying, embarrassing, important, etc.) thing that happened (on the job, in that situation, while you were a student, on the honeymoon, etc.).

- What happened that made you change your mind about that?

- Tell me about a situation in which you had to take an unpopular stand.

- Give me an example of why his (or her) mates feel that way about him (or her).

It is important to interview third parties about the main source because they can give you information and insights that might not emerge in your interview with your main source, who might be too modest or too reticent or too forgetful or too secretive or too embarrassed to tell you about something that turns out to be a gem in the finished story. Third parties can tell you such things. You can conduct interviews with third parties by telephone. You contact third parties solely to elicit information about your main source and you need not describe them or their surroundings.

These third parties may be the source's spouse, parent, child, friends, coworkers, enemies, supervisor, subordinate or anyone else who knows the source well enough to tell you stories about him or her. If you tell third parties you need some interesting little stories to flesh out the purely factual information about your main source, most will oblige. Get as many anecdotes as you can. You need many anecdotes because until you get to the writing stage, you won't know which anecdotes will fit the focus and be usable and which you will discard. So it's a question of getting as much information as you can from your sources.

THE IMPORTANCE OF BEING OBSERVANT

You must learn how to make best use of sources and documents and to make a special effort to be observant. The more closely you observe your sources and their surroundings, the more vivid will be your feature stories. In feature writing, the idea is to paint word pictures so vivid that you give your reader the illusion of standing next to you as you observe the scene. Since you lack the space for extensive description, you must select just the right details to establish the atmosphere and describe your sources and their surroundings well enough to give your reader the illusion of being there.

Look for the tiny, telling detail, the one that stamps the scene in some unmistakable, unusual, or even unique way. Being observant goes beyond noticing what colour clothes your source is wearing. Readers have five senses — sight, sound, smell, taste and touch — so when you write, you should appeal to as many senses as you can. You do this by writing about things that your reader is likely to be familiar with. Thus, when you paint your word pictures you conjure up memories for your reader, memories that enable him or her to imagine what you're describing.

Just as you describe the blue singlet, the red Stubbies and the heavy brown work boots, you also describe the photograph of the spouse on the desk; the rustle of the dry leaves underfoot; the aroma of percolating coffee; his sand-paper rough three-day beard; the salty oysters; the oily film oozing out of the ground; the greasy fingers from the take-away chicken; the chianti bottle with the melted wax running down the sides from the candle stuck in its neck; the table with the red-and-white checked cloth; the wisp of blonde curl she keeps brushing out of her eyes; the drip, drip, drip of the leaky tap; the threadbare carpet; the three letters missing from the brand name of the refrigerator.

It's not enough just to notice details like that. You have to remember them so that you can weave them into your story. This means that you have to jot down notes about them. An excellent time to do that is during those boring patches in the interview. You don't want to appear to stop taking notes because this might act as a damper on the interview. So you keep your pencil moving. But instead of jotting down what your source is saying, make notes to yourself about that checked tablecloth or that leaky tap. And, of course, you are holding your notebook so the source can't see what you're writing. Thus, you can put to good use an otherwise dead space in the interview.

YOUR DEMEANOUR WITH YOUR SOURCES

Try to see the world as your source sees it and accept things from your source's point of view. That doesn't mean that you must approve of what the source says or does or even that you must believe what he or she tells you. But it does mean that you must react calmly and matter-of-factly to your source's statements. It's usually a mistake to pretend or express surprise, shock, boredom or disapproval.

And never, never, ever, under any circumstances, argue with a source, no matter what the provocation. An interview is not an occasion for you to tell your source what you think. It is an occasion for the source to tell you what he or she thinks, and you can't learn anything while you're talking. You are not there to show your source the error of his or her ways or to convert your source to your way of thinking or to defend your journalistic integrity and professionalism. If your source verbally attacks you, you have to wear it and soldier on. An interview is not for you to talk. It is for you to listen. So listen, and listen well. Do not allow a source to draw you into debates. Do not give advice to a source. If a source asks you what you would do in his or her place, respond with something like, "This is your show. My job is just to report what you do. What are you going to do?"

By your questioning, convey that you know enough about the story to write it correctly. This is where backgrounding comes into it, and why it's important to know something about the topic and the source before you go for the interview. Be sure that you know enough so that you understand the questions you are asking. This means that you have to be able to translate the jargon of the source's field into language that the average reader can understand. Ask questions that the source is qualified to answer. Know what you want and go after it. Don't be afraid to ask what you want to know. If you don't ask, you won't get an answer. Ask questions to which you already know the answer. This is helpful in checking the accuracy of what your source is telling you, and it also gives you some breathing space if you need a little more time to write down the previous answer.

Ask the easy questions at the beginning of the interview. Save your big or embarrassing questions for the end. Then, if you get thrown out, at least you have answers to a lot of other questions and can still do a story. As well, watch for the change of pace answer, that little hesitation before the answer, during which you can almost hear the wheels turning in your source's head. If you hit a nerve, treat it like a big or embarrassing question: Go on to something else and come back to it at the end of the interview. If your source remains silent or says, "No comment" or something similar, like, "Look, I'm not going to be drawn on that", you can develop a story around the fact that so and so remained silent or declined to comment when asked such and such. Restrict use of this tactic to politicians or other genuine celebrities, though, because it doesn't really matter if a nonentity doesn't want to answer a question but a politician's or celebrity's silence might well be newsworthy.

If you want to get reaction to criticism of a source's views, play devil's advocate and distance yourself from that criticism. You want to avoid even the hint that you disagree with the source. Say something like, "I guess a lot of people would agree with you on that, but I've heard the opposite view lately. What do you say to critics who say you're wrong?" No matter what's been said, a lot of people probably would agree with it, so you're simply stating a fact that sounds like approval but isn't really approval. Then, when you get to the criticism, you pin it squarely on people who are not present so the source won't turn antagonistic toward you.

The main thing to remember about questions is that they must be fair. Loaded questions are out. Trick questions are out. This means you don't ask when he stopped bashing his wife. You don't ask questions with quadruple negatives hoping to trip her up. Keep the questions simple and short. Make it easy for your source to understand what you're asking. Ask questions that require only one answer, not compound questions requiring several answers. Compound questions are difficult for a source to keep in mind, and you might find that in answering some of the parts, the source doesn't touch on other parts at all. Never make it easy for your source to say no to something you want to know about, so phrase your questions positively, not negatively. In other words you ask, "Whose fault was it?" and not "You wouldn't know whose fault it was, would you?"

GOOD LISTENING AND OTHER STRATEGIES

The key to good questioning is good listening. Take your cue for the next question by evaluating the previous answer, even as you are listening to it. It's a good idea to use an answer as a springboard for the next question. It shows the source that his or her thoughts are really important, that you are really listening because you have processed the answer and thought of a follow-up question. This is much more flattering than simply peppering him or her with a barrage of questions all prepared before the interview.

Good listening includes letting your source tell the story in his or her own way. Don't interrupt the flow of an answer with the next question. Don't interrupt with interjections such as, "I know" or "I understand". If your source thinks you know or understand, he or she might stop. Allow your source to come to a complete stop in his or her own time.

When you think your source may be holding out on you, sit silently and look expectantly at the source for five or six seconds. This allows you to harness the extraordinary psychological power of silence. When one person is silent in a conversation, the other feels a compulsion to break the silence. Let your source be the one to break the silence. Sometimes in breaking the silence sources expand on the original answer and give you more information, and sometimes that information is better than what your source previously told you. But don't let the silence go on until it becomes an uncomfortable, strained silence. Before that happens, break the silence yourself with another question.

Silence is only one of the tactics you can employ to get your source to expand on an answer. As you have seen, open-ended questions accomplish this. Another method is to ask for examples or chronological accounts. Ask your source to take you through a process or an event step by step. If you're not satisfied with an answer, rephrase the question and ask it again. Author-Journalist Shirley Biagi reports that White House correspondent Sam Donaldson's favorite follow-up question is "Why do you say that"?[3] Try it.

Also try displaying your ignorance. In this ploy you deliberately misrepresent your source's position by asking a question or making a comment that tells your source that you have not understood something. You want your source to go to such great lengths to correct you that he or she tells you more than originally intended. This ploy can backfire, however, if the source thinks that you're so hopeless that he or she refuses to deal any further with you.

The other side of the ignorance ploy is the knowledge ploy. In this one, you feign knowledge to encourage a source to cooperate with you. All you have is a tip, but you pretend to know more hoping to open the source up. Sometimes it works, but this one, too, can backfire if the source tells you that since you already have the story, he or she can keep out of it.

You don't have to get every single word of a direct quotation. If you capture the key words, you can usually fill in the rest from short-term memory and from the logic of the language itself. To make best use of your short-term memory, get to your keyboard as soon as you can so you can flesh out your notes, particularly the direct quotes. If you find later that you cannot reconstruct a direct quote, you can always paraphrase it. If it's such a good quote that you want to use it as a direct quotation, telephone the source and say you're having a little difficulty deciphering your notes at one place in the interview. Perhaps if you prompt the source about the subject matter, he or she can repeat it for you.

GOING OFF THE RECORD

There are some conventions you should be aware of in handling information. You should assume that any interview is on the record, which means that you can use any of the information and attribute it to the source. But sometimes people don't want you to identify them as the source of information. They want to tell you things off the record.

Your first response should be to try to persuade the source to stay on the record. There are a couple of ploys you can use. You can tell the source, "Don't tell me. I don't want to hear it off the record. I want to remain free to write about everything I see and hear." Or you can say, "I have an idea what you're talking about and I think I can get someone else to give it to me on the record. So don't tell me". These tactics might induce the source to tell you the information on the record so he or she can put the "proper" interpretation on it for you.

Ultimately, you have only two choices when a source asks to go off the record. You can say yes or no. But you must be careful because the source might mean one thing by off the record and you might mean another. In 1989, Arthur Gorrie, then the AJA Queensland's president, tried to explain the concept in a submission to the Parliamentary Judges Inquiry.[4] Gorrie concluded that "off the record" might assume "a range of meanings" and might well depend upon "the understanding reached between the journalist and the source at the time of the interview". So before you agree to accept information off the record, reach an agreement with the source so that you're both talking about the same thing.

Generally, there are three levels of off the record, though there is not universal agreement about this point. The lowest level is that you can use the information but may not attribute it to the source in any way that could identify the source. You can attribute it in a way that conceals the identity of the source by associating the source with a large, anonymous group, as, for example, "an informed source" or "a person close to the mayor" or "a party official".

The middle level is that you can use the information unattributed, on your own authority, as background. This has the disadvantage of putting you out on a limb if the source is floating a trial balloon that he or she never has to acknowledge if it draws criticism. In other words, the source does not have to stand by the information he or she gave you. But you do.

The highest level is called deep background. In this case you may not use the information at all in the present. You are being told so that when something else, something major, happens, you will understand it better and can then use the off-the-record information. Again, your source may be taking you for a ride by co-opting your silence, never intending for the tempting later event to occur.

In actual practice, off-the-record transactions between sources and journalists are not clear-cut. In his submission to the judges, Gorrie said that the union thought a journalist could publish information given off the record by a source if the journalist could find another source who could provide the information. If a journalist were not free to do that, Gorrie wrote, sources could censor the news "simply by prefacing an interview with an 'off the record' proviso". Gorrie concluded: "This clearly is ludicrous and would muzzle freedom of the press."

Such a position is reasonable for the AJA to take, since one of the major obligations of a trade union is to look after the interests of its members. So in a dispute between a journalist and a source over the use of off-the-record information, you would expect the AJA to plead freedom of the press.

To my way of thinking, however, if you agree to take information off the record, you forfeit your freedom to use it. You bargain your freedom away. Keeping your word should be the overriding professional value when you take information off the record. You are honour-bound not to use it until your source gives permission. This means that you cannot use it even if someone else tells you on the record. Your original source will reach the altogether reasonable conclusion that you are dishonest and unethical, that you do not keep your word, that sources cannot trust you. Certainly that source will never trust you again and might even spread aspersions about your ethics. If a source has taken you in and has co-opted you, so be it. You have learned you cannot trust that source. Try not to let it happen again with other sources.

In my opinion, only if you decline to accept information off the record do you remain free to use it if you can get it from another source. The problem is that until you hear the information, you can't be sure how valuable it is, so you can't know whether the source is offering you the information to help you or to hinder you. You must be ever vigilant to prevent people from hindering you, so try to avoid accepting information off the record.

On the other hand, if you really do have an idea what it is, if you need it for background and if it's not important enough to spend time digging out, go ahead and accept it. Under those conditions, perhaps it's more important for you professionally to cultivate the source and to demonstrate your trustworthiness than it is to publish the information.

The most serious situation occurs when a source puts his or her job or even his or her life in jeopardy by leaking information to you. Public servants, backbenchers, even Ministers leak information that higher-ups want kept secret. And if the leaker is uncovered, he or she can be sacked or prosecuted. The Australian and State Governments routinely launch police investigations to find out who leaked sensitive documents to journalists. Much more rarely, an underworld informant risks his or her life by giving information about criminal activities to a journalist who publishes the information without identifying the source.

The AJA Code of Ethics currently in force requires journalists "in all circumstances" to keep confidential what they receive in confidence. That means that you run some alarming risks yourself if the information you accepted off the record becomes a topic for litigation or criminal proceedings. A judge might order you to reveal the name of your source. But once you have promised anonymity to a source, you are honour-bound to keep your promise. So under the present code your professional ethics might require you to disobey the judge and by doing so risk a fine or imprisonment for contempt of court.

In September 1995, a Journalists Ethics Review Committee brought down a revision for discussion by members of the AJA. That revision, if adopted, seems to qualify the requirement that "in all circumstances" a journalist keep confidences. The revision recognises that not every source acts from noble motives. It says: "Aim to attribute as precisely as possible all information to its source. When a source seeks anonymity, do not agree without first considering the source's motive and any alternative attributable sources. Keep confidences given in good faith." In other words, under the revised code of ethics, bad faith on the part of a source, such as lying, might release a journalist from a promise of confidentiality given in good faith to that source.

Despite the uncertainty and the pitfalls, taking information off the record is a normal journalistic activity. But make sure you think through all the ramifications when a source asks you to promise anonymity.

CONCLUDING THE INTERVIEW

When you feel that you have accomplished all that you can in an interview, signal that the end is near by saying something like, "Let me check my notes and see if I've forgotten anything". Then do just that and clear up any problems you find in your notes.

At this point, it's a good idea to give your source some input, so you ask, "Is there anything I should have asked you but didn't?" This protects you against missing anything important that you just didn't know about and also gives your source one last chance to initiate a line of thought. Work through any last-minute topics your source mentions. Then ask if you can telephone back if there's any further information you need or if you need to check on the accuracy of something.

Make a flourish of putting away your notebook and turning off your tape recorder. Thank your source, gather up your belongings and head for the door. But before you leave, linger for a few parting remarks. The interview is not over yet. Every so often you pick up something good as you're lingering at the door. If that happens, do not whip out your notebook or start up your tape recorder. Be cool. But keep what was said in your memory until you're out of sight, then jot it down. Now the interview is over.

[1] See Strentz, H. (1978) *News reporters and news sources: What happens before the story is written.* Ames: University of Iowa Press, for a comprehensive study of the reporter–source relationship.

[2] The importance of body language in interpersonal communication has long been recognised. This section applies to the journalistic interview concepts and conventions found in Pease, A. (1985) *Body language.* Avalon Beach, NSW: Camel Publishing Co., which is an excellent source for more information about how to read and use body language in other settings and for other purposes.

[3] Biagi, S. (1986) *Interviews that work: A practical guide for journalists.* Belmont, CA: Wadsworth Publishing Co. This is the best book on journalistic interviewing I have found, and I highly recommend it.

[4] Gorrie, A. (3 April 1989) Letter on behalf of the Queensland Branch Committee of the Australian Journalists' Association to The Secretary, Parliamentary Judges Inquiry.

Chapter 3
QUOTATIONS

Direct quotations add sparkle and life to any piece of journalistic writing, so a human-interest story should contain many of them. Organising your material preparatory to writing consists largely of selecting which quotations to use and working out which order to use them in. When you come to the writing, it's mainly a matter of picking up those quotes and deciding what you have to write by way of introduction, explanation and linkage. Because of the importance of quotations, then, it's well for you to learn how to handle them before you reach the writing stage. To gain maximum effect from direct quotations, you have to know how to select them, how to set them up to maintain the flow of the story and how to shift from one speaker to another.

SELECTING GOOD QUOTES

Writers write in paragraphs, but people do not usually speak in paragraphs. They jumble their words and speak in thought clusters that contain complete sentences, non-sentences, false starts, repetitions, redundancies, abandoned lines of thought and disconnected thoughts. From the dozens of thought clusters that you have gathered during your interviews, you have to decide which statements to include in your story as direct quotations and which as indirect quotations, or paraphrases.

Your focus dictates your selection decisions. All quotations, direct and paraphrased, that you will use in your story must fit your focus. This simplifies your selection problems immensely, because your focus enables you to discard most of what your sources told you.

Your first step is to identify and set aside for inclusion all the quotations that remotely fit your focus. You're just at the beginning of the organising stage, so you can afford to err on the side of selecting too many for inclusion rather than too few.

The best quotations are the ones that put things brightly or succinctly or interestingly, or uniquely. Look for quotations that illuminate your main source's personality, that show his or her individuality, that reveal insights about his or her feelings, attitudes, beliefs and behaviour.

PRUNING THOUGHT CLUSTERS

Many promising quotations will be unusable for various reasons, for example the speaker didn't finish the thought or made major grammatical errors. Most of the time you will have to prune rambling thought clusters to mine good quotations. But pruning is dangerous. You must be careful not to change meaning. On May 23, 1996, Prime Minister John Howard was responding to a political criticism that he had made a secret deal. He said, "If every proposal that I had put to me as an Opposition politician represented a secret deal, I can tell you that I made more secret deals than any other politician that Australia has ever seen." Clearly, it would be unethical and a monstrous misquotation to prune that quotation to just the last part: "I made more secret deals than any other politician that Australia has ever seen". Yes, he said it. But you must retain the qualifier to convey his meaning.

What follows is an excerpt from a transcript of an interview with Peta Ramsey, wife of a fundamentalist Christian pastor leading a ministry to rehabilitate street kids in Ipswich, Queensland. She was interviewed simultaneously with Eric Inch, her husband's colleague. They were discussing, reluctantly and cautiously, their fundamentalist Christian belief in the casting out of demons. For the purposes of this example, however, only Mrs Ramsey's thought clusters and the journalist's remarks are reproduced. The journalist's words are in italics. Following the transcript excerpts, you can see how her remarks appeared in the *Queensland Times*. Pay particular attention to the way the journalist discarded the vast majority of the information contained in Mrs Ramsey's thought clusters and plucked the chosen quotes from a welter of surrounding material.

> *One thing I've been picking up a little ... actually I've got quite a bit of information on it ... casting out of demons. Some of the kids have talked about their experiences to me. What I lack is authoritative information from people like you on that.*

What did you want to know?

I want to know what happens when demons are cast out. Well, let's back up. I want to know IF demons are cast out.

Scripture does talk about it. That's part of Jesus' ministry. He taught, he preached, he healed the sick and he released those that were in bondage.

Don't get me wrong. I'm not going to sensationalise this. But I think it's an important aspect of what the kids are being taught after they come in, after they make their commitment. And I think that's a legitimate part of the story.

We do have a policy on that. And our policy is that first and foremost we call people to know Jesus Christ as their Saviour. Because we know from our own personal lives that a knowledge of Jesus Christ and repentance of our past life and acceptance of Jesus Christ changes our life. And that does 95 per cent, if not 100 per cent of what we need in our life. Sometimes it's a past involvement in the occult, direct involvement, kids are influenced, people are influenced, and that might need to be repeated.

Influenced by?

Demonic influence, I suppose you'd call it. But our policy is that that's not the important part of our ministry.

(Eric Inch said that casting out a demon was a means to an end.)

Tell me what the end is, just for the record. Salvation?

Yes. Salvation is right. That's the end. Somebody's sick and they're healed. We don't jump up and down that they're healed of the physical ailment. We jump up and down that out of that God's glorified and their relationship with God is deeper. That's the aim.

Is healing the same as casting out a demon?

They have been related in Scripture. Like there was an epileptic and he had a demon cast out of him. We look at epilepsy and we'd say it's a sickness and we would treat it as a sickness. It's a complex subject. You're getting into a deep subject when you start getting on to … you know, and we don't consider ourselves expert in that field. But when you have a clash of the spiritual, the two opposing forces, and they come together, there's a reaction.

Tell me who the two opposing forces are.

Well, you know, the devil and Jesus.

I want it in your words.

Well, the opposing forces, on the one hand there's Jesus Christ and He shed blood and on the other side there's Satan and his attempt to bring us into bondage and death.

When you cast out a demon, how do you do it?

In the name of Jesus … It's certainly something that isn't recommended for everybody to go around trying.

It's been the most difficult area to probe.

It's just that it isn't the most important area. It's a ripple in the road. It's a ripple in the road. You're just going along and boomp, you know.

(Eric Inch said that casting out demons was not something they did for the sake of doing it.)

I understand that.

Yeah, because there is a school of thought that this person isn't doing something in their Christian life and they must have a demon and we're going to get this thing out of them. And that isn't it at all.

How do you know, then, when to do it?

I think that's something that it'll let you know. It'll let you know. Well, I did read something the other day. The expression they used was like when the clouds roll together and there's turbulence and as they come together there's a crash, a mighty crash. As the spirit of God is working and working, the Devil doesn't like it and pretty soon, snap, you get a reaction. Boom.

Here is how the material was used in the story:

Invoking the name of Jesus is the only way you can exorcise a demon, according to Inch.

"You can't do it in your strength," he said. "You've got to do it in God's strength, in His authority."

Inch and Peta Ramsey, the pastor's wife, both downplayed the practice.

"That's not the important part of our ministry," Mrs Ramsey said. "Our policy is that first and foremost we call people to know Jesus Christ as their Saviour."

But sometimes a demon impedes that policy, she said.

"When you have a clash of the spiritual, the two opposing forces, and they come together, there's a reaction," she said.

"On the one hand, there's Jesus Christ, and He shed blood, and on the other hand there's Satan and his attempt to bring us into bondage and death."

Inch said demons were cast out as a means toward the end of helping someone gain salvation.

"There's something holding him back," he said. "There's an area of their life, they've been mucking around with the occult or something, and they have been, what's the word?"

Possessed?

Inch: "I don't particularly like that word."

Mrs Ramsey: "Under influence."

Inch: "Yeah, under influence. By a spiritual force. Then God gives you the power, the authority, to do something about it.

"But it's not something you do just for the sake of doing it."

Mrs Ramsey agreed.

"It's certainly something that isn't recommended for everybody to go around trying," she said.

"There is a school of thought that this person isn't doing something right in their Christian life and they must have a demon and we're going to get this thing out of them. And that isn't it at all."

RETAIN CONTROL OF YOUR STORY

After choosing which quotations you are going to use, you have to decide further which to use as direct quotations and which as paraphrases when you write your story. Your sources have written much of your story for you with their direct quotations, so your contribution to the writing is the paragraphs that go between their direct quotations. It is not difficult to handle direct quotations and paraphrases, but beginning writers require much practice before it becomes second nature. Your exposition should provide springboards for colourful quotations.

Use direct quotations early in your story, especially from the main subject. After all, it is the main subject's story, so give him or her a starring role in its telling. In the writing, you have to strike a fine balance between direct quotations and paraphrase. Don't stifle your sources with too much of your exposition and paraphrase. If you do that, your story takes on the tone of a lecture to the reader. So let your sources speak liberally, let them have their say, let them tell their stories in their own words.

But don't overdo it. Don't use paragraph after paragraph of block quotations. If you do that, you relinquish control of your story to the speaker. *You* must retain control, so keep a tight rein on a source. Don't let a source ramble unless what he or she is saying is so controversial that you want to make sure that the information is unmistakably pinned to the source, or unless you are deliberately making a point about the source's talkativeness.

Remember that you must write relentlessly to your focus. It is highly unlikely that long quotations from a source spoken in the context of an interview will fit your focus as precisely as a mixture of your exposition and direct quotation will fit it. In general, to keep to your focus, use exposition that leads into short and snappy direct quotations.

Show, don't tell, with quotations

Direct quotations are important in illuminating a subject's personality because they show word choice and patterns of speech. How a source talks *shows* the reader the main subject much more effectively than mere exposition or description from you can *tell* the reader about the main subject. Use of direct quotation, then, is an important aspect of the technique of showing the reader, not just telling the reader. This is particularly true if the direct quotation reveals emotion. It is more dramatic to hear the emotion in the subject's own words, in the subject's own voice, than to hear *about* the emotion from you in your impersonal, third-person, objective voice.

Here's an example of an instance where a writer used third-person where direct quotations would have been better, assuming that usable direct quotations were available. The story was about Colin Scotts, who was trying to become the first Australian to succeed in American football, what Aussies call gridiron. Seven paragraphs into the story, the writer had just said that 120 players begin training camp, where that number will be cut to the 45 players each team is allowed to nominate to begin the season.

> **As Colin Scotts has learned with much pain, becoming one of the chosen 45 is survival of a totally different dimension.**
>
> **It's having an enraged 300 lb veteran (in American football, every player becomes a veteran after his first year) striving to preserve his place and fearing the opposition of this handsome Australian, tearing off the front of Scotts' mask.**
>
> **It's enduring the pain that comes from the ordeal of twice daily training when every man, the veterans and the new players, strives to stay in the race to be one of the final 45.**
>
> **And it's surviving the emotional hurt of waking up to find under your door a goodbye note from a fellow rookie who has become a friend, given his marching orders.**

It's a shame that the writer used third-person in those paragraphs. The third-person accounts are vague and unspecific. They lack the authenticity of first-person accounts. The awesome sight of an enraged giant ripping an iron facemask off a gridiron helmet simply doesn't come through in the third person. What did Scotts think at the time? What was his reaction? What words does he choose now to tell the reader about it? What exactly takes place during those twice daily training sessions during which all players struggle to be among the chosen 45? How did Scotts react to them? What words does he choose now to tell the reader his recollections of them? The emotional hurt of the disappointed rookies is bland and too matter-of-fact coming from the writer. Scotts should describe it to the reader so the effect of their hurt on him can come through. In short, what happened in this story was that instead of showing the pain and the hurt through Scotts' direct quotations, the writer told the reader about them in the third-person. Far better to use direct quotations.

SETTING UP QUOTES FOR YOUR READER

Before you use a direct quotation, write an expository paragraph that sets it up, that foreshadows it. Foreshadowing is important because you want the coming quotation to advance the foreshadowed thought, to maintain the story flow and therefore to advance the story. It is easy to set up a quotation, but it does take a little planning. The easiest way is with a word bridge. A word bridge is a linking device between two sentences. Used properly, a word bridge provides transition from the last few words of your expository paragraph to the first few words of the quotation.

The first two sentences of the previous paragraph are linked by a word bridge: "foreshadows" in the first sentence is echoed in the second sentence by "foreshadowing". Repeating a word or a related concept is a common way to write a word bridge between two sentences. Likewise, the previous two sentences in this paragraph are bridged by "echoed" and "repeating". So you can see that it is not difficult to link your expository paragraph to the direct quotation you have selected. It's just a matter of keeping the thought flowing through use of related words or concepts at the end of one sentence and the beginning of the next.

Because you know the first few words of the direct quotation you have selected to use next, it is easy enough to write the preceding expository paragraph so that it ends in a word bridge. Thus, your exposition reads smoothly into the quoted material, and you have maintained the story flow. But in your set-up paragraph don't just use the same words as the upcoming quotation. If you do that, you turn your source into a parrot and instead of advancing the story you bog the reader down in repetition.

Beyond its role in advancing the story, the set-up is important because it provides the context in which the reader encounters the quotation. Because you conducted the interview, you know what the context was, so all the quotations make perfect sense to you. But the reader was not at the interview, so the reader's only context is the one you provide on the page. Setting up the quotations provides a context for the reader and makes it easy for the reader to follow your story.

Keep your story moving forward

Your story should move along at its own pace and according to its own momentum. It's all right to move back and forth in time, of course, as long as such movements are made clear to the reader and as long as they advance the story you are telling. But you should never back up in a story. This means that you should never go over the same ground twice.

For example, you should never have to explain what a source meant by a quotation. If you have to explain a quotation immediately after using it, you have failed to set it up properly in the first place. Your failure to provide the context forces the reader to think back to what the source has already said. Instead of advancing your story, then, an improperly set up quotation bogs it down and may stop your reader.

Another way you can bog down the story is to write a set-up that does not foreshadow the appropriate quotation. Here are two examples where young writers did this. In the first case, the set-up said that a museum worker received job satisfaction from seeing her finished product. But in her ensuing quotation she said that she received satisfaction when other people had seen the finished product and mentioned it to her. And in the second case, the set-up said that in taxidermy the eyes had to be placed correctly so that they did not look comical. But the ensuing quotation said that the hard part was trying to make a run-over animal look alive. These set-ups told the reader to expect one thing, but the ensuing quotations delivered something else. The reader is left behind, the flow has lapsed, the story has bogged down and the reader may stop.

Vary the voices telling your story

One way to maintain reader interest is to vary the voices that tell the story. Direct quotations from a number of people provide the variations. The most commonly heard voice, of course, is your own third-person voice as observer, narrator and story teller. But too much of your voice makes for a dull story in which the reader is simply being told things and is a passive listener. You don't want the reader to feel passive. You want the reader to feel that he or she is actively participating. You accomplish this illusion by shifting the centre of attention as different speakers take the spotlight.

You shift the centre of attention by providing transition when you change speakers. This keeps the reader informed of the dynamics of the word pictures you are creating. You do not want sources just bobbing up and speaking in your stories. Smith has just been quoted. You intend to shift to Jones for a quotation.

Just as in the real world you turn your attention from Smith to Jones as Smith finishes speaking and Jones is about to begin, so in the world of your word pictures you turn your attention from Smith to Jones. Signalling that a different speaker is about to take up the story gives your reader the impression of being in a three-dimensional word picture where attention shifts from speaker to speaker as in real life. This gives your reader the illusion of looking from one to the other, the illusion of participation. Always confirm to your reader that a shift in speakers has taken place by providing attribution after the new speaker's first sentence. And, of course, when you shift the centre of attention to a new or a different speaker, you should also set up the ensuing quotation so that the story maintains a smooth flow.

Let's look again at that excerpt from the *Queensland Times* series on street kids. This time view it as an example of good quotation set-ups and smooth shifts back and forth between the sources, Eric Inch and Peta Ramsey. The journalist attempted to place the reader at his shoulder, watching and listening, as the two sources went back and forth in their discussion of a subject they were not comfortable discussing with an outsider. The first transition shifts the centre of attention to Inch from a street kid who had just been quoted as saying he had rebuked a demon in the name of Christ.

The shift to Inch is economical with a word bridge that provides the set-up for his upcoming quotation, for which attribution is provided at the end of the first sentence.

> **Invoking the name of Jesus is the only way you can exorcise a demon, according to Inch.**
>
> **"You can't do it in your strength," he said. "You've got to do it in God's strength, in His authority."**
>
> **Inch and Peta Ramsey, the pastor's wife, both downplayed the practice.**

The third paragraph is a signal that the centre of attention is shifting from Inch to Mrs Ramsey. The set-up foreshadows that she will downplay the practice.

> **"That's not the important part of our ministry," Mrs Ramsey said. "Our policy is that first and foremost we call people to know Jesus Christ as their Saviour."**

The attribution after her first quoted sentence confirms to the reader that she, and not Inch, is now the speaker. Next comes a paraphrase pruned from unused (and unusable) direct quotations about involvement with the occult and demonic influence, with the "impedes"/"clash" concepts providing the bridge.

> **But sometimes a demon impedes that policy, she said.**
>
> **"When you have a clash of the spiritual, the two opposing forces, and they come together, there's a reaction," she said.**
>
> **"On the one hand, there's Jesus Christ, and He shed blood, and on the other hand there's Satan and his attempt to bring us into bondage and death."**

Next comes a shift back to Inch as the speaker. Again the set-up foreshadows his direct quotation and immediate attribution confirms the shift. What follows is a quick back-and-forth groping for just the right words to describe this sensitive subject. The journalist depicts the short exchanges while always making sure the reader knows who is talking. Notice how unobtrusively the journalist contributes to the exchange with that unattributed, unquoted provocative suggestion: Possessed?

> **Inch said demons were cast out as a means toward the end of helping someone gain salvation.**
>
> **"There's something holding him back," he said. "There's an area of their life, they've been mucking around with the occult or something, and they have been, what's the word?"**
>
> **Possessed?**
>
> **Inch: "I don't particularly like that word."**
>
> **Mrs Ramsey: "Under influence."**
>
> **Inch: "Yeah, under influence. By a spiritual force. Then God gives you the power, the authority, to do something about it.**
>
> **"But it's not something you do just for the sake of doing it."**

Another shift back to Mrs Ramsey is extremely short. It looks like a throw-away line but it must be there to shift the centre of attention away from Inch and back to her and to foreshadow her upcoming direct quotation.

Mrs Ramsey agreed.

"It's certainly something that isn't recommended for everybody to go around trying," she said.

"There is a school of thought that this person isn't doing something right in their Christian life and they must have a demon and we're going to get this thing out of them. And that isn't it at all."

By way of contrast, here is an example of a good introduction of a new speaker but a poor set-up and use of her quotations. The story was about a man who went on a shooting rampage in Melbourne, and while the hard-news story was written under deadline conditions, the importance of smooth shifts to new speakers and set-ups of quotations comes through.

A policewoman at the scene said the gunman, who was near the railway station, was firing at anything that moved.

"He was shooting at anything that moved — we were hiding behind a tree while he was shooting," the policewoman said.

"He was shooting at police, shooting at ambulances, shooting at everyone."

The journalist did a good job of shifting the centre of attention from third-person exposition to the policewoman's first-person quotations. But the quotations were not set up properly. Instead, the policewoman immediately repeats virtually word for word the part of her direct quotation that the journalist had appropriated for the set-up. The flow of the story stops and the drama falters while the reader gets bogged down in needlessly repeated material.

In the following revision, pruning and rearranging the policewoman's direct quotations maintain the story flow and permit the drama of the moment to come through to the reader.

A policewoman at the scene said the gunman, who was near the railway station, was firing at anything that moved.

So far no change from the original.

"He was shooting at police, shooting at ambulances, shooting at everyone," the policewoman said.

"We were hiding behind a tree while he was shooting."

By pruning and rearranging the quotations, the revision thus makes the set-up foreshadow the rest of her quotations. Instead of merely repeating the set-up, the policewoman's quote now picks up the thread from the exposition set-up and verifies it. The journalist thus invites the policewoman to share the story-telling and makes the best dramatic use of her words. Rather than bogging down the reader in repeated words, the writer has taken the reader into the action of a vivid word picture. The reader is drawn closer and closer into the picture. The reader started watching the action from afar in exposition but the writer quickly sent the reader off to join the policewoman behind that tree.

Now that you have learned how to select and handle quotations, you are ready to use them and other tools and techniques in putting your story together from start to finish. The next chapter deals with leads and endings.

Chapter 4
LEADS AND ENDINGS

The lead or intro of a feature story has two primary functions — to attract attention and to set the focus. Only secondarily must it provide concrete information about the story. Obviously, you must connect the lead and the body, but this connection can be a loose one. In fact, you can use suspended interest to withhold the connection for a couple of paragraphs to pique the curiosity of readers. Suspended interest is such an effective device that most writers use it with any type of lead.

IMPORTANCE OF THE LEAD

Most writers find that coming up with a lead is the most difficult part of writing feature stories. In feature writing you don't have the news values to guide your choices and you always gather too much information in the wide-ranging interviews. So before you can write your story, you must sift through your material carefully and systematically.

The recommended system is an extension of the contributions of Goffman and Oldham. Goffman conducted research into "frames", which he said people use to answer the question "What is going on here?" to enable them to interpret the environment. Oldham applied Goffman's theories to the study of the frames journalists use in their work. She extended Goffman's question to: "What is going on here *that is newsworthy*?". And in a short chapter on feature writing in my textbook *Reporting and Writing News* published by Prentice Hall Australia, I modified Oldham's question to: "What is going on here *that is entertaining or interesting*?".

How you answer the feature frame question tells you which story you will write from your information and how you will entice people to read it. Your story must come to life in your very first sentence because newspaper readers are skimmers, spending less than 20 minutes with their daily newspaper. As well, newspaper pages are designed to encourage the eye to skip around amongst headlines, photographs, puzzles, comics and advertisements rather than settle on, say, your feature story. Therefore, you must arrest a potential reader's attention in your first 20 words.

DECIDING WHICH RHINOCEROS TO WRITE

But before you begin to write, you must answer the feature frame question on the basis of the information you have gathered, then organise your material accordingly. In other words, you must refine and hone the proposed focus that guided the path of your information-seeking. But you've returned with information you couldn't have anticipated in the early stages, and you want to include some of it in your story. So with the search for a new, refined focus in mind, sift through your information and come up with an answer to the frame question. Test each item of information against the focus you are now considering. This will allow you to discard information you know you won't need or to fiddle with your emerging focus so that information you wish to include will fit it.

As a rule of thumb, you'll discard 75 per cent of the information at hand. This means you'll use only 25 per cent. Think about that for a moment. If you have gathered 100 pieces of information and you use pieces one through 25, you'll write a much different story than the story you can write with pieces 50 through 74. Or suppose you use 25 odd-numbered pieces of information, or 25 even-numbered pieces. You see? Your options are astronomical. Which story will you write? Refining your focus helps you decide.

Years ago I read somewhere about a sculptor who was asked how he fashioned a statue of a rhinoceros. He replied that it was easy, he just got himself a block of marble and knocked off the bits that didn't look like a rhinoceros. Now his rhino could emerge from that block of marble in any direction, in any position, at any angle and at any size. All the decisions were in the hands of the sculptor. As a feature writer, you have to be like that sculptor. You have to decide which story you intend to write from the 100 pieces of information that make up your block of marble. You do that by knocking off the bits that don't look like the rhino you're writing, by deciding which 75 per cent of your information doesn't belong to that particular rhino, by deciding which 25 per cent does belong.

THINK BEFORE YOU WRITE

You should organise your material in the order you intend to use it before writing a lead for it. The more time you spend in this aspect of the process, the better off you are. Most good feature writers "live" a story they are working on. During the reporting stage and before they begin the actual organisation activities, they constantly think about the story and rehearse it in their minds. So by the time they start to sift through their information, they have a fair idea of where the story is headed. The more time you spend organising, the less time you'll need in the actual writing because you will already have some idea about where the story will go, and this will give you clues about how to start.

Writers divide into at least three schools on lead writing. Writers of the first school cannot write the second paragraph until the first paragraph says exactly what it has to say to set the focus. If they stray from their focus, they immediately go back and revise the first paragraph to make the focus cover the territory they have strayed into. Then they rework what they've written to ensure that everything fits the new focus. By contrast, writers of the second school can skip the first paragraph, write the whole story, then come back and write a lead that covers everything in the story. And writers in the third school write their first draft in one burst without regard to focus, spelling or any other consideration, then go back and fix it up on subsequent drafts.

As it happens, I am the first kind of writer. You will discover which kind you are as you gain experience in feature writing. Try any routines that occur to you. Most good writers use routines and rituals that help them get started. Only you can determine how you best can settle into the task at hand, so use whatever routines and rituals work for you and don't worry about how other writers get down to business.

Whatever kind of writer you are, do not be surprised when writing leads raises your stress levels. It is not unusual for a good feature writer to go through a couple of dozen false starts on a story. They are willing to go through that agony because the lead is that important. You must be able to shake off the frustrations of false starts and not let them hold you back. Whatever your routine, you must eventually get the lead exactly right. You must make it say precisely what is needed to tell the story. This will take time. You will probably find that your mind leads you into byways that are unfruitful. Or you will become obsessed with an approach and stick with it much longer than you should, trying desperately to twist it into saying what you want it to say.

Through all this frustration you must remain calm and leave your mind open to fresh ideas and approaches. Always be prepared to abandon an approach that isn't working, no matter how clever or cute you originally thought it was. In searching for a fresh approach, let your mind wander through the human interest and incongruous aspects of your information. Let the creative half of your brain play around with the information you have gathered. Turn the creative half loose early to search for the intro, and bring in the logical half in the latter stages to organise the story and interweave factual information.

Your first job is to hook the reader. You have many options. Adopt the playwriting technique of starting just before something important happens. Convey a sense of urgency. Use suspended interest by withholding vital information. Foreshadow a problem, then use a flashback to provide an explanation. Devices such as these enable your lead not only to make its promise, but also to set the focus and hook readers. Your lead should make it impossible for someone not to read the second paragraph. Then the writing techniques in the body will keep the reader with you through to the end.

The best feature leads are short. A lead less than 20 words long is good. One less than 15 words long is better. One less than 10 words is outstanding. This is so because the primary function of the feature lead is to attract attention. Short, stark statements attract attention. Long complex sentences don't. A short sentence creates suspense. It pulls the reader up. It packs a wallop. You want your reader to cast his or eye on your first paragraph and think "CRIKEY!" That will compel the reader to proceed to the second paragraph and, you hope, on to the end.

EXAMPLES OF FEATURE LEADS

What follows are some examples of leads. Here's an excellent news feature lead taken from Brisbane's *Courier-Mail*:

Stephanie Ryan is trying to pick up the threads of her life.

The writer has given the reader precious little information, only that someone named Stephanie Ryan is trying to come back from an unspecified adversity. As a news lead, it would be inadequate because it lacks detail. But this lack of detail is precisely what makes it superb as a feature lead. First, it attracts attention by keeping the reader in suspense and hinting at what the story is about. Second, it conveys urgency. Third, it foreshadows a problem. In the next few paragraphs, the writer unfolded the story of a young woman left for dead after a knife attack and of how she was trying to put her life back together.

There are a number of ways to approach a feature lead. The Stephanie Ryan lead is pure suspended interest because it draws the reader into it by giving only a little information but implying much more. Below are examples of other approaches, but note how all use suspended interest.

You can start with incongruous information to startle or intrigue your reader. You hope to pull your reader up short and entice him or her to think about something from an unusual perspective. Here's an example from a news feature about a deadly subject:

> **The AIDS scare has reached the point where a man advertising for a flatmate recently specified that applicants had to prove they were not AIDS carriers.**
>
> **And the Melbourne-based Pacific Dunlop Ltd reported an AIDS-inspired bonanza in Australian and US sales of a subsidiary's latex gloves for medical and dental use.**
>
> **But, strangely enough, sales of its condoms in Australia did not increase, despite a 25 per cent increase in other countries.**

The thrust of this story obviously will be the AIDS scare and the writer used three pieces of incongruous information in the lead paragraphs to illustrate some reactions to the scare. The first paragraph goes longer than 20 words but it contains two ideas — the AIDS scare and the man's advertisement. Notice that the slight subjectivity ("has reached the point") grew out of the writer's interpretation of the fact of the placement of the advertisement, not from foisting an opinion on the reader. The second paragraph objectively reports an increase in the sales figures for some anti-AIDS paraphernalia. The third paragraph makes a subjective interpretation ("strangely enough") of the fact that there was no increase in the sale of condoms in Australia. The story continued:

> **It is strange because medical experts agree that you cannot catch AIDS through casual contact with a carrier or a patient.**
>
> **The principal ways that you can catch AIDS are through the exchange of body fluids — particularly through sexual activity and even more particularly through receptive anal intercourse — and through infected blood, particularly on a needle used to inject drugs into yourself.**

So, unless the man advertising for the flatmate thought he might enter into a sexual relationship or shoot up heroin with the successful applicant, he might have saved himself the advertising cost of the wordage regarding the AIDS test.

And all those doctors, dentists and nurses purchasing all those latex gloves won't need them for the vast majority of the patients they touch, though of course they should take precautions when handling the fluids and wastes of AIDS carriers and patients.

And people who have sexual relationships with AIDS carriers, especially those people who have anal intercourse, might well be advised to insist that the penetrator use condoms, as the national AIDS Taskforce says that the use of condoms "is likely to greatly reduce or eliminate the risk".

You will learn more about writing in the feature style in the next chapter, but it's useful to take note now of some of the devices and techniques used in these few paragraphs. The writing is informal, almost conversational, and there is repetition ("And *all those* doctors, dentists and nurses purchasing *all those* latex gloves"). There is alliteration ("casual contact with a carrier"). The writer addresses the reader directly as "you" to increase reader involvement. There is parallel construction, with consecutive paragraphs beginning with "And".

The fourth paragraph imparts factual information, quoting experts to the effect that the precautions described in the first three paragraphs are likely not to be effective. The fifth paragraph is also informative and factual, telling how "you" can catch AIDS. And the sixth, seventh and eighth paragraphs clean up the flatmate, gloves and condoms motifs in the same order as they were introduced, all containing objective information laced with some subjective interpretation of fact.

Here's a lead that uses description and also contains suspended interest:

Mary Ryan has several hundred freckles north of her waist and she works in a place where you can count them as you sip your drink.

The story was about the first bar in New York City to employ bare-breasted barmaids. In feature stories you can take a casual, relaxed approach that includes colloquialisms, slang and unusual constructions, such as "north of her waist" instead of "above her waist".

Here's a lead that uses personification, a play on words and suspended interest:

Chi-Chi said no-no to An-An today.

The story was about the London zoo's unsuccessful attempts to mate giant pandas. The attempts failed because Chi-Chi wouldn't have anything to do with An-An. The writer bestowed a human touch on this sexual rejection through the whimsical use of "no-no".

Here's one that uses a parody and suspended interest:

Once a jolly swagman camped beside the Brisbane River.

Such leads are rare, hence this one's a made-up example. The idea of leading with a parody is to lull the reader into expecting something very familiar but putting a sting in the tail that delivers something else. You use a lead like this to call attention to similarities and differences between a real-life occurrence and some familiar literary work, such as a quotation, a saying, a poem, a novel, a television program or a motion picture.

Here's a lead by Juanita Phillips of the *Courier-Mail* that uses a third-party anecdote about the main subject:

> **Two years ago a work colleague transferred to Melbourne was jogging gamely, if sluggishly, through Royal Park. One by one, a seemingly endless stream of glistening bodies overtook him without a word.**
>
> **"Suddenly this dreadfully fit man drew alongside me," he recalled. "He smiled, looked me in the eye, and said 'G'day, mate', before running on.**
>
> **"It was Bob Ansett. He was the only jogger who ever said hello to me."**
>
> **The vignette says as much about Ansett as it does about joggers.**

Using an anecdote automatically employs suspended interest, since the point of the anecdote is at the end. Ms Phillips used the jogging anecdote well to *show* her readers something about Ansett instead of just telling her readers. As you already know, this is an important aspect of feature writing. Leading with an anecdote is a good approach because of an anecdote's ability to "hook" a reader. If the little story at the beginning is interesting, a reader is likely to enjoy it and read the whole story.

Notice that leading with an anecdote breaks our rules about writing short leads and putting the focus in the first sentence. Don't worry about rules. Your first job is to be creative, so in feature writing you can break any rule you like except the one about falsifying facts, as long as your rule-breaking serves a particular function within your story. Naturally, you have to have a good grasp of the rules before you can break them. You can't break them out of ignorance or sloppiness, only for effect. You can even use such devices as incomplete sentences and improper grammar.

PROVIDE THE "WHY" WITH A PROCESS LEAD

Another type of lead is one that I call a time one/time two lead. Usually it's the kind of lead you see on a story in which someone has turned his or her life around, either coming from the bottom to the top or from the top to the bottom. It's a lead that typically says something like:

> **Five years ago Joe Bloggs swept up behind the elephants in a traveling circus. Today he is the president of the state investment advisers' organisation.**

To my way of thinking, a lead like that contains suspended interest and makes a promise all right, but it leaves out the most important element in the transformation of the individual — the thing that brought about the change. In other words, the interest is *too* suspended, the promise is *too* vague. I much prefer what I call a process lead — one that takes into account the transformation of the individual but also includes the reason for the change. So a process lead would say something like:

> **The loneliness of dull motel rooms led Joe Bloggs from a life of sweeping up after circus elephants to the presidency of the state investment advisers' organisation.**

The focus is thus shifted from the mere fact of change to the "why" of the change, which is much more interesting. And plenty of suspended interest remains to pique the reader's curiosity about Joe Bloggs' career change.

QUOTATION AND QUESTION LEADS

Two other common types of leads are quotation leads and question leads. I think both are weak approaches and should be avoided, especially by beginners. Sometimes beginning writers use a quotation lead or a question lead as a crutch because they are unsure of themselves and are reluctant to make a decision. In the case of quotation leads, rather than take the risk of picking something out of their information and leading with it, beginners instead pick out their best quotation and stick it on the top of their story. The second paragraph almost always says something like "Joe Bloggs said this after he ..."

In the case of the question lead, beginners are overwhelmed with their information and cannot decide what is important and what is not. So they start with what they think is the key question, and they then proceed to answer it. There are two main problems with a question lead. First, a journalist's job is to answer questions for the reader, not pose questions to the reader. And second, if the question is a yes/no question and the reader answers "no", the reader likely won't go on to the second paragraph.

The problem with leading with a quotation is that the reader has no idea who is speaking, and so cannot judge the importance or validity of what is said. Moreover, the reader encounters the quotation in a vacuum and therefore has no idea of what is being talked about. The usual quotation lead says something like "It was the worst thing I ever saw!" Now those words could cover a multitude of situations, from the dismissal of Gough Whitlam to the bombing of Hiroshima to the loss of Balmain to Canberra in the rugby league grand final, depending upon who is making the evaluation. So the promise made in such a lead is too vague and doesn't give enough information to hook the reader.

Having said all that, let me confess that I have read at least one quotation lead I thought was good. In fact, I thought it was wonderful. It was written by Karen Allan, a QIT journalism student. Here it is:

> **"The saddest thing for me is that I will never be able to teach my mother's language or her history because it has all been lost with the genocide of my people."**

That quotation lead worked because it clearly indicated that the speaker was a teacher and it reflected the anguish at what he or she considered the deliberate extinction of his or her heritage. Exactly who the speaker was seemed unimportant at the beginning of this story because of the universality of the racist implications of what was said. It could be Everyperson poignantly crying out against every injustice ever perpetrated by one group of human beings upon another.

Let me also confess that despite my criticism of question leads, I found myself writing one for the last story in my eight-part series on street kids. I did everything I could to avoid writing a question lead. In all my years as a senior journalist, I had never found it necessary to resort to one. But after writing seven articles on the street kids, it was time to write the concluding article, one that would sum up the problem and offer solutions.

I spent two days wrestling with the problem of how to begin a story dealing with those issues. In the end I could not come up with a focus broad enough to cover everything I wanted to cover in the story. So I reconciled myself to writing the first question lead I had written since my very early days as a journalist. It asked: "Is there much hope for Ipswich street kids?" Bad enough it was a question lead, but it was a dreaded yes/no question lead. The only thing it had going for it was that it did provide a broad enough focus. As I said, you can break any rule you like for functional reasons. That question lead allowed me to bring in a larger number of opinions than ever could have been encompassed by a more conventional focus. And the series was highly commended, so perhaps question leads and quotation leads aren't as bad as I generally think they are.

UNLEASH THE CREATIVE SIDE OF YOUR BRAIN

In moving from the lead to the body of the story, many writers try to get the first draft of the story out of their heads and onto the computer screen as quickly as possible, in one sustained creative burst of writing. They do this to take advantage of the creative side of their brain. They want to start their creative juices flowing and keep them flowing until that first draft is down. So they don't stop to correct spelling errors, they don't stop to make sure every little fact is correct, they don't stop for anything. They know they can bring the logical side of the brain into play later to fix things up. During the laying down of the first draft they give their creative side free reign.

They do this because the creative side is anchored in the unconscious, unhampered by the inhibiting conscience, the ego. Your story has been percolating in your unconscious since the first germ of an idea formed. And unleashing your unconscious mind is what creativity is all about. That's where your conceptual leaps are made, that's where your most perceptive observations come from, that's where your deepest and most significant truths lie.

EXAMPLES OF FOCUSES THAT WENT ASTRAY

What follows are criticisms of more than 50 beginners' feature stories that had misleading focuses. As you read through the examples, note the kinds of mistakes that beginners make and be aware of how they were advised to improve their efforts. If you keep these common errors in mind, your leads will provide proper focuses for your reader.

- The lead said the woman was so busy that her daughter had to make appointments to see her but there was no evidence in the story that the woman was busy. The story *said* several times that the woman was busy, but the reader was never that she was.

- The first paragraph said the story would be about old-fashioned values but the story never mentioned them again.

- The lead said how hard it was to run a particular business, but the story never mentioned any difficulties in running that business.

- The lead said his job required him to use a lot of skills, but many jobs require the use of a lot of skills. Write a lead that is unique to your story.

- The lead said the woman has immense talent and enthusiasm but the story merely made it clear that she tried hard.

- The lead said the politician wanted to be a minister so he could implement his policies for conservation but the story never mentioned what conservation strategies he had in mind.

- The lead said a private boys' school was changing by hiring women teachers, but the story was about one interesting teacher who happened to be a woman. Because of her sex, interesting and frustrating things happened to her on the job.

- The lead said there's more to the wedding ring than the reader might think. How can the journalist know what the reader might think? Is the journalist a mind-reader? The journalist should just find some facts and report them, not try to tell the reader what he or she should think.

- The lead said that the word "condom" conjures up a certain image. Again, how can the journalist know what is conjured up in someone else's mind?

- The lead said that a house made of bottles was a famous tourist attraction. If it's famous, you don't have to tell the reader. If it's not famous, your calling it famous won't make it famous. Lead with something new about it so the reader can recall past knowledge.

- The lead said it would be hard to imagine the exciting adventures about an outback teacher. How can the journalist know what is hard for a reader to imagine? As well, there was nothing in the story about exciting adventures.

- The lead said that a feminist said that women who aspire to be equal to men lack ambition. Nothing in the story supported that assertion.

- The lead said that a househusband was not what you might expect. Passing over the mind-reading trick on the part of the journalist, don't take up space telling the reader what the subject is NOT. Write positively. Tell what it is, not what it is not.

- The lead said that some of Brisbane's finest assets were housed in a particular museum but the story contained no evidence to document that assertion.

- The lead said that a woman had to choose between art and history but the story never again mentioned that choice.

- The lead said the interviewee was wearing a clown's nose and the story never again mentioned it, so the reader never found out why he was wearing it.

- The lead said she was the queen of her suburb but the story gave no evidence that this was so.

- The lead began with description and the main source did not appear in the story until the second page. What newspaper reader would hang around that long to find out who the story's about?

■ The lead said that it took a special person to do a particular job. You could say that about any job. Write a lead that is uniquely about your story.

■ The lead said that a teacher tried hard to motivate children to stay at school, but the story never showed the reader how she did that.

■ The lead said many students find it difficult to find jobs during the school holidays and very few enjoyed the jobs they did find. Passing over the mind-reading, this story was not about a student who had trouble finding a job he liked. It was about a student who had a holiday job he loves waiting for him.

■ The lead said the original owners of some city property wouldn't believe their eyes if they saw it today. Of course they wouldn't. No one from the 19th Century would believe their eyes if they suddenly found themselves in the late 20th Century.

■ The lead said that every little girl wants to grow up to be a famous actress. More mind-reading. The story should have focused on the actress it was written about.

■ The lead said that people who are retired, or who are housewives, or who hate gardening or who want to meet people could work at what the man in the story did. None of those types was mentioned again in the story. The story should have focused on that man — who worked as a lollipop person at a school crossing.

■ The lead said that the man succeeded as a radio announcer because he failed as a musician. This construction is known as a *non-sequitur*, which translates from the Latin into roughly "does not follow". It does not follow that because he failed at music he succeeded as an announcer.

■ The lead mentioned that his mother wanted him to be a doctor and that fact was not mentioned again until the last paragraph.

- The lead said that she was a single parent who ran an introduction agency from her home. The story was not about the problems faced by a single parent in a situation like that. In fact, the story had nothing to do with her being a single parent. Her youngest child was 25 years old and living on her own.

- The lead said it sounds like something out of a science fiction movie. More mind-reading. You can't assume readers will think like you. Besides, you're supposed to describe only what you detect with your five senses, not what you think.

- The lead said he sold costumes but didn't know how to sew to create them. So what? Does a menswear salesman know how to tailor suits? Does a petrol station attendant know how to refine petrol?

- The lead said that withdrawal from tranquilisers is worse than withdrawal from heroin. The story never documented that assertion.

- The lead said that the driving aim of most women was control of their own fertility. Passing over the mind-reading, the story was about a pill that causes abortions in the second trimester of pregnancy.

- The lead said there was a push for a return to public examinations for Year 12 students in Queensland. The story was about complaints about the present system from two anonymous teachers and a defence by a board spokesman.

- The lead said the great Australian dream was to own a home. But the story shifted to people trying to build homes, then shifted again to the problems faced by a specific young couple trying to build a kit home.

- The lead said something about vermin extermination. The story was about a company that captures possums from people's roofs and returns them safely to the wild.

- The lead asked what kind of person buys a feathered mask. The story never answered that question.

- The lead said a person's face echoed with the stride of rush-hour pedestrians. I don't know what that means.

- The lead said he overcame his father's disapproval. The story was a rather straight-forward account of a man who had been successful in several fields.

- The lead said students who drop out of uni and then go back have problems. The story was about what a girl did while she had dropped out of uni.

- The lead said he was torn between music and acting. The story was about his successes as an actor.

- The lead said something about 350 migrants, 12 countries and 25 languages. Too many numbers. It should have said something short and snappy about the subject.

- The lead said that most people would label a woman who did certain things insane or a witch. More mind-reading.

- The lead said the source would be the first to admit that he is an extrovert. A lot of people could make that statement. Lead with something unusual about that person.

- The lead said that a piano was mechanically amazing. I don't know what that means.

- The lead said that goldfish were an alternative to messy budgies and expensive dogs for people who wanted to keep a pet. The story never again mentioned budgies or dogs, so the focus should have been on goldfish, not on some comparison with other kinds of pets.

- The story said that facsimile machines had revolutionised business and would soon be found in people's homes. Nowhere in the story did the writer explained how fax machines work.

- The story was about a ghost. But the ghost did not appear in the first paragraph, nor was the reader ever told her name or the circumstances of her death that led to her haunting the building.

- The lead said an old theatre was getting a facelift, but the story then went into a chronological history of the theatre with the facelift not mentioned again until the last paragraph.

- The lead promised a story about the evolution of the cigarette, but the story wandered off onto the health problems caused by smoking and the difficulty of stopping smoking.

- The lead said that Dr Martens boots were linked with youth fashions and musical trends but although the story documented the link with fashions, nothing more was said about music.

- The lead talked about panicking when a bright light swept across your house or car, then wandered off into arrests and UFOs. These are straw men dragged into the story to provide a forced bit of drama because the writer couldn't think of a good way to start a story about a piece of Expo 88 sculpture, Night Companion, that contained a beacon light that swept through 360 degrees.

- The lead said that XXXX beer had been associated with Queensland for a long time. Ho hum. The story was about Bond Brewing caving in to Queensland's renowned parochialism by removing its Perth corporate address and restoring the Brisbane address to the labels of XXXX cans, stubbies and bottles.

- The lead tied an introduction agency concept to the television program *Perfect Match*. But the story never explained how the television game worked and how the introduction agency was similar.

- The lead mentioned a muttaburrasaurus. A word like that is likely to stop a reader cold. Much better to talk about dinosaurs or prehistoric monsters to draw the reader in, then bring in the scientific terms.

- The lead mentioned a person who never again appeared in the story. You know you're on the wrong track when a person you mention in the lead is irrelevant to the story.

- The lead talked about a new wave in the tide of sexual freedom but the story was a history of contraception starting with the ancient Egyptians.

- The lead talked about the new roller coaster, but the story never showed the reader what it was like to ride it. Strap the reader into the seat, then take him or her on that ride metre by metre. Feel that long, slow, jerky, tense crawl to the top, that first sudden drop that leaves your stomach somewhere above you, that loop-the-loop, that zoom to the end. What do you see while you're upside down and screaming, by the way?

- The lead asked what you do when you walk into a dark room. The answer in the second paragraph was that you'd turn on the light. Would you bother to read the third paragraph? I wouldn't. Any writer who thinks I'm so stupid that I wouldn't know enough to turn on the light has very little to offer me. The story was about the development of electricity.

- The lead said that new legislation would end shonky practices in a certain industry. Perhaps, but it's safer to say that the new legislation was aimed at shonky practices.

- The lead mentioned a pro-smoking group. Now an anti-smoking group is pretty well-defined as a group opposed to smoking for health reasons, advertising tobacco products and sponsorships from tobacco companies. But what is a pro-smoking group? Does it try to get people to start smoking? Does it advocate smoking?

- The lead said that people were rejecting the use of technology and turning to alternative health therapies but the story was about the conflict between exponents of traditional and alternative medicine.

- The lead said that the Ahern Government was attempting to bring about a Queensland-style glasnost. The story was about proposed legislation that would permit women to prosecute their husbands for rape within marriage.

ENDING YOUR STORY WITH A CIRCLE

Because the lead of a feature story is not a summary, a feature story must have some sort of resolution in the final paragraph, just as any narrative must have. Virtually any ending that brings the story to rest will suffice, but I prefer circular endings because they round off the story as well as resolve it.

In a circular ending, your final paragraph echoes something mentioned in the lead. This echo can be a repeated key word or a concept that is closely related to a concept in the lead. Your reader thus begins with the lead, goes through the body of the story, then is brought back to the lead. The paragraphs in the story should be so tightly linked that your reader feels a sense of satisfaction at the end, a sense that everything has been resolved, a sense of resolution and completeness. A well-written circular ending provides the illusion of a never-ending story.

Here are some examples of leads of stories and their circular endings. In each case several hundred words separated the two paragraphs.

Lead: **Both boys had been drinking rum and sniffing petrol.**

Ending: **So they stay on the streets. And mess up their lives even more, with alcohol, drugs, sex and crime.**

Lead: **Three kids a day lob into Life Line looking for a place to sleep.**

Ending: **And three new kids a day show up on Life Line's doorstep looking for a place to sleep.**

Lead: **When Pastor Jeff Ramsey talks to you in his quiet, reasonable voice, confidence and sincerity flash from his penetrating pale blue eyes.**

Ending: **Hence the confidence and the sincerity in his eyes.**

Lead: **The Ipswich street kid problem is largely but not entirely a parenting problem.**

Ending: **Better than their parents.**

Lead: **Street kids can find support among Ipswich police officers.**

Ending: **Dancing with kids or arresting them, many Ipswich police officers try to be supportive.**

Lead: **Pastor Jeff Ramsey and his born-again Christians figured that God would show them how to save the street kids of Ipswich.**

Ending: **But the ROAM volunteers remain convinced that the pot is stewing according to God's recipe.**

Lead: **Some Ipswich street kids are learning to maintain constant vigilance to keep God in their hearts and Satan out.**

Ending: **And the born-again Christians are working hard among street kids to keep him out and to invite God in.**

Lead: **Is there much hope for Ipswich street kids?**

Ending: **So rays of hope do break through. But there are hundreds of kids out there.**

Lead: **It is quite a switch when a journalist sits down for half an hour with another person and they talk about the journalist.**

Ending: **Who wouldn't be happy? Sitting down for half an hour and hearing all about yourself. It's only human nature.**

Lead: **The police enjoy going to your party about as much as you enjoy having them there.**

Ending: **In the end they decided not to return. But in making that decision, they were risking having to return later with much less help to try to arrest people likely to be drunker and even less co-operative.**

Lead: **The police sped to a house expecting to find a son threatening his mother with a knife.**

Ending: **So the real troublemaker was the one person in the house not mentioned in the radio call.**

Lead: **Zooming past the Ipswich night traffic in a police car at 100 kmh "keeps your heart young', a constable remarks later.**

Ending: **Those uncertainties are a part of the job that a constable soon learns to deal with. But as for that middle-aged passenger in the back seat hanging onto the cage for dear life, well, his heart might be staying young, but his hair surely must be getting greyer by the kmh.**

Now that you have learned about leads and endings, it's time to learn how to write the stuff that goes between them.

REFERENCES

Goffman, E. (1974). *Frame analysis*. Cambridge: Harvard University Press.

Granato, L. A. (1991). *Reporting and writing news*. Sydney: Prentice Hall Australia.

Oldham, C. J. (1986). An analysis of the frames reporters use to identify newsworthiness. Unpublished PhD thesis. Lexington: University of Kentucky.

Oldham, C. J. (1988). "Framing" Australian journalists: Research in progress. *Australian Journalism Review*, 10, 170–1.

Chapter 5
THE BODY

The body is the structural backbone of the feature story. Throughout the body of the story you must fulfill the promise that you made in your lead. The story must move smoothly from the lead through the body to the ending. Each paragraph should validate the focus. In other words, nothing should appear in the body that has not been foreshadowed in your focus. With your focus as your underlying theme, let your story unfold naturally and simply so that you lead your reader step by step to the ending.

Your reader should never have to work hard to follow your story. But to save your reader from having to work hard, you have to work hard. It is not easy to tell a story naturally and simply. You have to utilise several writing techniques to ease your reader's task and to maintain his or her interest. And you must make your efforts seem effortless. Otherwise, your writing will call attention to itself and detract from your content.

This chapter will discuss some techniques that will ease the way for your reader. These techniques all serve the general and critical function of showing your reader, not merely telling your reader. The techniques are (1) providing peaks and valleys; (2) modifying the inverted pyramid; (3) using the second-person "you"; (4) writing in block paragraphs; (5) spiraling; (6) telling anecdotes the way people tell jokes; (7) pruning quotes that ramble; (8) describing people, settings and processes; (9) backgrounding people; and (10) revising. All these techniques help you lead your reader through your story.

As noted, all these techniques help you show your reader something, not merely tell your reader about something. Showing is what good, vigorous writing is all about. Showing requires you to paint vivid word pictures that come to life and draw your reader into them. You run the risk of losing reader involvement when you merely tell the reader about things in your exposition or narrative. By merely telling, you make your reader a passive receiver of information that you are imparting. And just as a student's attention wanders in a boring lecture, so does your reader's when he or she loses involvement in your story. The worst thing you can do as a writer is to bore your reader. So show your reader key aspects of the story instead of merely telling your reader about them. Of course you must also tell about things, but when you do, follow up immediately by showing an example of what you just told your reader about.

PROVIDE PEAKS AND VALLEYS FOR YOUR READER

Along the way, provide little peaks of suspense and little valleys of resolution. You must have noticed how television writers create little peaks of suspense just before each commercial break. These peaks keep the viewer interested and willing to pick up the thread of the story after the commercial break. Immediately after the commercial break that little bit of suspense is resolved and the play moves on to the next peak just before the next commercial break. You, too, have to keep your reader's interest from flagging. So create little problems — little peaks of suspense — and solve them for the reader. Such devices are "hooks" to keep the reader interested in learning what will happen next.

MODIFY THE INVERTED PYRAMID

You have considerable leeway in the writing because feature stories are more informal and relaxed than straight news stories. Features modify the fabled inverted pyramid format of newswriting in which facts are presented in order of their decreasing importance. The format is modified to take advantage of the greater freedom afforded in feature writing by the narrative writing technique. Whereas in newswriting, using the rigid inverted pyramid, you organise your material in order of importance according to traditional news values, in feature writing you organise your material in order of importance to fulfilling the promise you made in your focus. By thus thinking in modified inverted pyramid terms, you should organise your material so that you tell in some logical fashion the story you promised in the focus.

You would not ordinarily tell your story in chronological order because you want to convey a sense of drama — tension and conflict. The "Once upon a time" approach will not do that. So do not place history or background high in your story. Rather, you should start by telling your reader something new about the subject and put any history and background later. A good place to start is just before something important happens. Get a sense of urgency into your first sentence to pique the reader's interest and curiosity about what happens next. While you might tell some aspects of the story in chronological order for ease in understanding, the story should unfold topically as you fulfil the promise of your focus.

ADDRESS YOUR READER DIRECTLY AS "YOU"

In keeping with the traditions of story telling, the language of feature stories is informal and conversational, even chatty, as opposed to the impersonal, detached third-person approach of straight newswriting. The idea in a feature story is to write with "voice", that is, to give your reader the illusion that you are talking directly to him or her, and only to him or her. As you write, think of yourself as writing for only one reader, one with whom you hope to establish a warm, friendly atmosphere in which to tell your story.

Toward that end, it's a good idea to address your reader directly, by using the second-person "you" rather than the third-person "one". The second-person "you" establishes an informality that the third-person "one" can never match.

You undoubtedly have noticed that I have been using this technique constantly in these pages, particularly in this chapter. I have consciously and consistently been talking to "you" about "your" reader, not "the" reader. I do this to take advantage of the benefits of the conversational, chatty approach and to encourage you to feel that I am talking only to you. Here's an example from a newspaper feature story:

> **Rolf Harris is not quite what you expect.**
>
> **He does not come charging in wobbling his wobble board, blowing his didgeridoo.**
>
> **He is suddenly there, next to you, and he looks like the bloke down the street, but a very nice bloke down the street.**

The writer has utilised the "you" technique quite well to create the illusion of chatting directly to one reader about the well-known Aussie entertainer. Then, because the reader likely has seen Rolf Harris on television or on stage wobbling his wobble board or blowing his didgeridoo, the writer calls up those images in a

71

word picture and thus shows the reader something new about Rolf Harris. And in the third paragraph the writer skillfully paints the word picture promised in the focus: Rolf Harris is not what you'd expect, he's like your very nice neighbour. Thus, the writer has shown Rolf Harris to the reader by coupling the informality of the "you" technique with two familiar word pictures: (1) the frenetic Rolf Harris onstage that "you" probably remember, and (2) the very nice neighbour down "your" street.

Another way to show your reader and personalise your story is through your use of direct quotations. Direct quotations are your single most powerful writing technique in feature writing. They provide change of pace and variety from your "voice" and style and illustrate the "voice" and speaking style of the person being quoted. This change of pace and the appearance of another "voice" in the story break the monotone of your narrative by changing the patterns, word choices and manner of speaking. As well, direct quotations let your sources share the work in carrying your story forward.

BLOCK WRITING AND SPIRALING

Two other devices that help you keep your story moving forward are block writing and spiraling. In block writing you place related material in contiguous paragraphs. Exhaust one topic before moving on to the next one. If you do not write in blocks, you scatter information about a topic in different parts of your story. Scattered information gives your reader the impression of backing up because he or she encounters familiar material instead of new material. And if your reader has the sensation of backing up, your story obviously has ceased to move forward.

When you spiral your writing, you use transitional devices such as word bridges, conceptual bridges and linking words and phrases to make each paragraph lead into the next. Avoid providing natural stopping points along the way by keeping your story moving. The idea is to pique your reader's interest again and again to encourage him or her to keep reading and to discourage him or her from putting your story down. So when your reader finishes one paragraph or block, a transitional device spirals your story into the next paragraph or block and so on until the end of the last sentence.

Here is an example of block writing and spiraling, taken from the street kid series. In the previous block a youth worker had expressed doubts about whether the dole and other social welfare services really helped street kids because of their

feeling that society doesn't really care about them. The youth worker had said that
street kids were reluctant to "come there" to seek help.

> **Sometimes when they come there, they find the cards stacked
> against them, as a 15-year-old blonde discovered when she
> reported problems with one of her many foster fathers.**

The word bridge "come there" spirals the story from the youth worker block
to a block about problems encountered by a 15-year-old girl. So the story has thus
moved from a valley as the youth worker concluded his remarks to a new peak of
suspense in a new block. The transition paragraph introduces the girl as the next
speaker and leaves the reader hanging on the information that she found the cards
stacked against her. No stopping point here, as the writer has encouraged the reader
to stay on to find out about the girl's problems and why the cards were stacked
against her.

> **"Finally I spoke up to my welfare officer and they couldn't
> believe me," she said bitterly. "You're a kid. Why should
> someone believe a kid?**
>
> **"Who wants to believe a kid when they've got an adult saying
> a different thing? The adult is always right. The kid is always
> wrong."**
>
> **She has found fellowship with Ramsey's born-again
> Christians.**

That block finishes with her specific validation of the youth worker's
generalisation about street kids not finding help from welfare agencies and her own
frustration about being sloughed off by her welfare worker. Then the story spirals
toward the next block. The 15-year-old's peak settles into a valley with "found
fellowship". Note that the girl's real-life problem has not been resolved. Only the
tension created in the writing about it has been resolved. The writer has created a
peak, then a valley. Then the transition paragraph announces that a new block about
Ramsey's born-again Christians will begin.

> **The Christians are happy to accept the kids into their own
> circle, but they do not measure their success in terms of
> increasing their own flock, as Peta Ramsey, Jeff's wife,
> explained at the beginning of their street kid ministry.**

This is a transition paragraph to the new block. The word bridge "Christians" spirals the writing from the girl. And the paragraph introduces Mrs Ramsey as the next speaker and creates a little problem for the reader (how do the Christians measure their success, if not in terms of increasing their own flock?).

> **"We try to integrate them into any fellowship we feel they can relate to," she said back in March. "We are not just trying to win a convert to our church so we can say we have one more member. We want to help each person develop their full potential."**

Her direct quotation resolves the little problem and brings this block to a close. By now you should be expecting a transitional paragraph to the next block. Here it is:

> **One 16-year-old girl, a member of the Ramsey flock, became a Christian in 1984 when she went to a Christian camp.**

This time the spiral is a conceptual bridge (a member of the Ramsey flock, a Christian). The transition paragraph introduces a new speaker and foreshadows her quotation (she will tell us about becoming a Christian).

> **"They introduced me to God," she said seriously.**
>
> **Then she grinned and her eyes sparkled with mischief as she continued:**
>
> **"And it was really good, ay, I learned how to ride a horse and everything."**

That quotation and the description of her grin and sparkling eyes showed an aspect of the girl's personality and finished off her block. The story then spiraled to a new block with a transitional paragraph that took up another aspect of the Christians.

TELL ANECDOTES LIKE JOKES

Quotations can also help you show your reader things by the way you relate anecdotes. During the interview stage you dutifully collected many anecdotes. Now you need to weave some of them into your story. Since anecdotes play a major role in personalising your story, you must plan carefully how to use them. You will recall from the chapter on quotations that sources speak in thought clusters that you must prune. This means that precious few anecdotes can be inserted into your story just as they were told to you during the interview. So expect to do a lot of pruning when it's time to use an anecdote.

A good way to tell an anecdote is to tell it as if you were playing second banana in a comedy duo. This ancient technique of joke-telling can be useful in telling an anecdote, even though you're not always after a laugh. A joke has two parts — the build-up and the punchline. Comedy teams use the second banana to draw the listener in with the build-up. Then the top banana delivers the punchline. While the punchline packs the ultimate wallop, a proper build-up is essential for the punchline to work.

And so it is with anecdotes. Your task as the writer is to be the second banana and provide the build-up. Then you let the source be the top banana and chime in with the crucial, climactic punchline. The anecdote is, after all, the source's story, so he or she should have the honour of delivering the punchline, of conveying the anecdote's climax. You will find that it is relatively easy to write the build-up. You can paraphrase much of what the source said in his or her own build-up to the anecdote during the interview.

Moreover, in this pruning and paraphrasing, you can shape the anecdote so that it suits your present purposes, to illuminate something about the subject and to keep the story on focus and moving. Remember that the source did not have those purposes in mind when he or she told you the anecdote, and at that time you probably didn't know how you would use the anecdote, or even if you would use it. But now, in the writing stage, you know precisely what you want that anecdote to accomplish for you. And you're the writer. You can build it up quicker and better in paraphrase than the source did in direct speech.

When you paraphrase you can cut through any rambling and over-kill and make the build-up say what you need it to say, always remembering, of course, that you must remain true to the source's meanings and that you must attribute the information to the source. Write the build-up so that it builds a little peak of suspense for the reader, just as a second banana does in the build-up to a joke. Then, when you have the reader hanging on a peak, you switch play to the source, who delivers the punchline in direct quotation and thus provides a valley of resolution. Then write a transition spiral to the next peak of suspense.

This method helps you maintain maximum control over your story. Liberal use of direct quotations relieves the monotony of your narrative "voice", gives your reader the illusion of several voices telling the story and shares the story-telling with your sources, so when they read the story, they will find themselves occasionally in the spotlight. But remember that when you shift to direct quotation, you effectively turn over control of the story to whoever is speaking. Although it's a good idea to use a lot of direct quotations, you must never relinquish control of the story to a rambling source.

Earlier you saw how a 16-year-old girl's anecdote about becoming a Christian appeared in a story. Here it is again. This time, however, you'll see how the information appeared in the interview, with the journalist's questions in italics, then how it appeared as an anecdote in the story, with the journalist writing the build-up to make it serve his purpose and to allow the source to deliver the punchline.

> *How old are you?*
>
> Sixteen.
>
> *Have you left school?*
>
> Yeah. Left school last year.
>
> *Do you still live with your parents?*
>
> No. No. I live with my foster parents. So what do you want to know?
>
> *Well, what do you want to tell me?*
>
> I don't know. What do you want to know?
>
> *Are you a Christian?*
>
> Yeah.
>
> *When did you become a Christian?*
>
> September two years ago. September 84. Late September 84.
>
> *How did you happen to become one?*
>
> I went to a horse riding camp. It was a Christian camp. And they introduced me to God. And it was really good, ay, I learned how to ride a horse and everything.
>
> *How long have you been coming down to the bus?*

I don't know. A couple of months now. Since it first started coming in town, I think.

There was more to the interview but you've seen enough of the transcript for present purposes. Here is how the anecdote connected with the previous block in the story:

> **The Christians are happy to accept the kids into their own circle, but they do not measure their success in terms of increasing their own flock, as Peta Ramsey, Jeff's wife, explained at the beginning of their street kid ministry.**
>
> **"We try to integrate them into any fellowship we feel they can relate to," she said back in March. "We are not just trying to win a convert to our church so we can say we have one more member. We want to help each person develop their full potential."**
>
> **One 16-year-old girl, a member of the Ramsey flock, became a Christian in 1984 when she went to a Christian camp.**
>
> **"They introduced me to God," she said seriously.**
>
> **Then she grinned and her eyes sparkled with mischief as she continued:**
>
> **"And it was really good, ay, I learned how to ride a horse and everything."**

The purposes of the anecdote in furthering the story were to follow on from Mrs Ramsey's assertion that her group sought to integrate street kids into appropriate religious fellowships and to show the impish quality of this teen-ager's recollection of her conversion. Note how the journalist paraphrased some of her unimportant direct quotations to write the build-up. He included in the build-up: (1) that the person was a girl, (2) that she was sixteen, (3) that she became a Christian in 1984 and (4) that her conversion occurred at a Christian camp. Then he switched to her for her two-part punchline divided by up-close description of her mischievous grin.

CUTTING THROUGH THE VERBIAGE

Human nature being what it is, a person telling you an anecdote often becomes over-helpful. You have asked someone to help you by telling you an anecdote, and you have given him or her your full attention. The source is naturally flattered by your reliance on him or her and by the importance you have placed on the anecdote in your general scheme of things. Such a friendly source is likely to tell you much more than you'll want to know, and in a roundabout way. In a genuine desire to be helpful and to make sure you understand perfectly, he or she is likely to tell you every little nuance and every little detail and wander off into verbal byways.

Here's an example. You'll see the anecdote first in the transcript of the interview, then in the story. The anecdote emerged during an interview conducted for a series on the human side of police work. As it turned out, the anecdote did not appear in any of the five stories that made up that series but found its way into the street kids series, which had not even been conceived when the interview took place. This aspect points up the importance of transcribing your important and lengthy interviews into computer files, from where you can retrieve them. Because that police officer's quotes had been saved in a file, the journalist could retrieve them by using the search function of the word processing software. Senior Constable Trevor Albury was reminiscing, and as he reminisced, he rambled.

> I've been in this town 19 years and I'm still running into people I worked with at the railway workshops. I'm running into their kids now. They were little kids when I worked in the workshops and now they're adults, teen-agers on the streets today. So I can say, "I know your father. I might talk to him about you." It puts the fear of God into them.
>
> Sometimes it's "How you goin' Trevor?" as you're going past.
>
> *(At this point Albury ordered the younger driver to park the car to provide back-up for another police team that was making an arrest. A young girl called Albury out of the car and engaged him in a short conversation. When he returned to the police car, he resumed his conversation with the journalist.)*
>
> The one with the short black hair has problems with her father. She hasn't spoken with him for four months. She's 16. She wants to go back to her father but is hesitant about going back. When

she approaches him, he always gets hot under the collar. She wants somebody to talk to him, to put a bit of sense into him. She wants to come home. she just lives in flats around town.

When you've been here a fair bit of time you get to know the kids in the street and they sort of rely on you for back-up and support. Dave Palmer was in Juvenile Aid for years, and he had a lot of respect from the kids. If they had a problem, they'd go and see Dave. A prosecutor here ... the kids had a lot of respect for him. They'd come into court and he'd help them through the court cases, even though he was the prosecutor.

Albury continued to ramble in that vein for some time. And while the journalist used some of what he said in the police-work series, the anecdote about the girl practically demanded inclusion in the street kids series. Here's how it appeared, beginning with a transition paragraph that spirals from the Christians to Senior Constable Albury.

Besides Jeff Ramsey's Christians, the kids have other friends on the street.

One of them is Sen. Constable Trevor Albury, who has been on the force for eight years. He has a lot of time for kids.

On the night I rode in Albury's mobile unit, two youngsters called him out of the car to tell him their troubles and, presumably, to ask his advice.

That was impressive. The kids wanted to talk to the copper.

"The one with the short black hair has problems with her father," Albury explained. "She hasn't spoken with him for four months.

"She's 16. She wants to go back to her father but is hesitant about going back. When she approaches him, he always gets hot under the collar.

"She wants somebody to talk to him, to put a bit of sense into him. She lives in flats around town. She wants to come home."

A lot of kids out there want to go home. And can't.

So they stay on the streets. And mess up their lives even more, with alcohol, drugs, sex and crime.

Note how the journalist plucked the anecdote from surrounding material in the interview, how he used virtually all of Albury's direct quotes because of their poignancy and dramatic impact and how he reversed the order of the last two sentences to provide a spiral to the ending of the story. Note also how the journalist told the reader in the build-up a generalisation that Albury had a lot of time for kids, then showed the reader by describing how two kids called him out of the car to talk to him. When he turned the story over to the top banana for the punchline, the use of extensive direct quotation showed that Albury knew the details of the private torments of the girl.

Although you want to use a lot of direct quotations, be careful to use them mainly in short bursts. Do not turn control of the story over to a source for an extremely long direct quotation unless the source's exact words are unusually dramatic, or poignant or controversial and therefore say it better than you could write it in exposition. In the above example, Albury's quotes about the street kid's problems with her father were much more dramatic and poignant than any exposition could have been, so the journalist let them run longer than usual. Generally, though, don't let a source go on too long, for fear of bogging the reader down. Instead, prune quotes into crisp paraphrases that keep the story moving and bring your sources in for relatively short direct quotations that are unusual, sparkling, sharp, pithy or controversial.

Here's an example of an unusual, sparkling quotation. Note how the journalist writes the build-up for the anecdote, then turns the story over to the source and keeps out of her way as she explains in highly individualistic fashion how she became a Christian.

One of the street kids who came home to God is another 15-year-old blonde, a friend of the pregnant girl.

The two of them went along to Ramsey's church one Sunday.

"I just thought Christianity was Christianity, it was a lot of, a lot of, um, well, crap," she said at the prayer meeting.

"We went to church for a laugh. And I ended up peaking out to the max. I'm sitting there oh! wow! man, what's happening?! We ran out.

"And I became a Christian sitting on a sewerage pipe."

DESCRIBE, DESCRIBE, DESCRIBE

Just as people have individual ways of speaking, they have individual ways of looking and acting. They assert their individuality by how they dress, how they wear their hair, how much make-up they use, how they sit, how they walk, how they carry themselves, how they relate to other people, how they feel about things, how they furnish and decorate their personal space. Good description conveys people's images and their personalities. So a good writer describes people's traits.

Good description comes from the writer's careful observation, not from the writer's interpretations. You should never try to tell the reader what to think about anything. Your job is not to instruct the reader but to provide observations that allow the reader to make his or her own interpretations and draw his or her own conclusions.

You can do this if you write in specific terms, not in generalities. Zeroing in on specifics is part of showing your reader, not telling your reader. When you write in specific terms, you convey information clearly and objectively. Information thus conveyed is more easily understood by readers than information conveyed by writing that meanders in vague generalities. This is because each reader will bring his or her own interpretation to a generalisation.

So the more specific your information, the easier you make it for your reader to visualise what you're writing about. For example, when you write that it is red-and-white *checked* tablecloth you are being more specific than if you just write that it is a red and white tablecloth. You thus leave less to your reader's imagination and enable him or her to identify better with what you're writing about.

Of course, you cannot always avoid generalisations, but when you find that you must write one, follow it up immediately with a specific example to enable your reader to test his or her imagination against the reality you are describing. So if you write that your interviewee has a good sense of humour, follow that general observation immediately with a specific example of his or her sense of humour.

Here are some examples of description based on careful observation, displayed here in isolation. Later in this chapter you will see how they fit into the stories in which they appeared. The first two examples are descriptions of people.

> **This time a solidly built man, bearded and dressed in a black leather jacket and tattered blue jeans, tapped him on the shoulder and invited him to come away from the bus.**

> **A 16-year-old brunette, stone cold sober, sits on Ramsey's bus. Eyes downcast, she pastes religious stickers in her Bible and tells you in her soft sing-songy voice that she ran away from home when she was 14.**

The next example is a description of a tense scene.

> **His friend was also bleeding. He had busted a knuckle wide open and blood was running down his right middle finger, dripping onto his clothes and the pavement. His right hand was swelling rapidly. He was having trouble closing it. He walked up Bell St to get away from his friend's abuse.**

And the final example is a description of a process.

> **When Gibson fingerprints you, she holds you firmly by the wrist and rolls your finger sideways on the inkpad, then rolls it in the proper square on each of four forms, always in the same order.**

> **She is systematic, starting with the little finger on one hand and proceeding in order to the little finger of the other hand.**

> **The police also take your palm prints and, in one print, all four fingers on each hand.**

In your descriptions include the source's surroundings — the home or office where the interview took place. Be selective. Since you can't describe everything, select aspects that will tell the reader something about the source: the photograph of the spouse on the desk, the ship in a bottle on the bookcase, the best actress award on the piano. But don't just describe what you can see. People have five senses you can appeal to, so also describe tastes, smells, textures and sounds. And be specific. Provide up-close details. The more specific your description, the more realistic your word pictures. And the more realistic your word pictures, the easier it is to involve your reader in them.

Here are two examples of up-close reporting and description. The first example is the first 15 paragraphs of the fifth story in the street kid series.

> **Street kids can find support among Ipswich police officers.**

> **Even when the kids are in trouble with the law.**

Seven young males and one 16-year-old female were arrested and charged with disorderly conduct one night.

This was on the first of three nights I rode with the police last March, and the eight kids had been arrested by officers in another unit.

Constable 1/c Barbara Gibson had been scheduled to go on mobile patrol at 10pm, but the necessity of having a woman police officer available to search and fingerprint the girl kept Gibson and her partner out of the patrol unit for an hour.

I was supposed to ride in Gibson's patrol car, so I watched while she booked the girl.

It is all done with observation. There is no interpretation. It starts with a generalisation that street kids can find support among the police. Then comes follow-up specific information. Notice the attention to detail: seven males and one 16-year-old female; the charge was disorderly conduct; on the first of three nights; other officers made the arrest; Gibson was supposed to start patrolling at 10pm but she'll be an hour late; she's about to book the girl, and the reader is at the journalist's shoulder watching as the journalist watches.

When Gibson fingerprints you, she holds you firmly by the wrist and rolls your finger sideways on the inkpad, then rolls it in the proper square on each of four forms, always in the same order.

She is systematic, starting with the little finger on one hand and proceeding in order to the little finger of the other hand.

The police also take your palm prints and, in one print, all four fingers on each hand.

Note how the sudden shift to present tense verbs adds to the immediacy of Gibson's actions. They seem to be happening right now, as the reader looks over the journalist's shoulder. Through careful observation, the journalist leads the reader in great specific detail through an experience he or she likely has never had — how the police fingerprint someone they have arrested. Then the centre of attention shifts off Gibson with a transition paragraph that describes the atmosphere. You should expect description that shows you the atmosphere.

The fingerprinting of the eight young people took place in a light, easy-going atmosphere.

There was good-natured back-and-forth chatter and joking between the kids and the police, even on the subject of the kids' being in the watchhouse.

The officers were friendly and helpful. They made sure each kid knew the options available on the disorderly conduct charge.

Bail was $40. If the kid wanted to contest the charge, he or she could appear in Magistrate's Court the next morning and get the bail money back.

If found guilty, the kid would be fined and a conviction would be recorded. However, if the kid decided not to show up for court, the bail would be forfeited but no conviction would be recorded.

One kid didn't know what "forfeit" meant so one of the officers carefully defined it for him.

Through careful, up-close reporting, paraphrasing and description, the journalist has taken the reader into the watchhouse for a look at what happens there when kids get arrested. The focus says that even when kids are in trouble with the law, they can find support among the police. The paragraphs of specific information that follow all restate the focus in some way. The fingerprinting sequence shows the kids in trouble with the law, and the description of the atmosphere and the paraphrased explanations show the support the kids receive from the police.

The second example of up-close reporting and description comes from the opening paragraphs of the first story in the street kids series. Again note how the journalist paints word pictures to take you to the scene.

Both boys had been drinking rum and sniffing petrol.

They were 15. And very drunk.

One was so furious and so frustrated he punched a plate glass window.

The glass vibrated and bowed ominously but did not break, to the relief of the four people sitting under it, including a woman in a wheelchair.

The story starts with a sense of urgency. No little peak of suspense here, we're immediately plunged into high tension. Something important is about to happen. The journalist pays attention to detail: two drunken youths, one of them furious; a plate glass window that bows; four people, one in a wheelchair, relief that it did not break and shower them with glass. The journalist was obviously there and puts the reader in the scene with vivid word pictures.

> **The kid was furious because his friend had walked up to a
> total stranger and for no reason at all had belted the guy in
> the mouth.**

Some explanation for the fury of one of the youths, obviously gleaned from overhearing their conversation and told in breezy, slangy, informal language.

> **"Man, the ****'s bleeding! He's bleeding! Man, you can't
> ****ing hit ****s like that!" the kid who punched the window
> screamed.**

A graphic example of that conversation, with not too much imagination required to fill in the asterisks, and use of "screamed" as the verb of utterance to help paint the word picture.

> **His language alarmed and alerted several born-again
> Christians who were providing free coffee and tea from a
> double-decker bus and who are engaged in a month's-long
> project to reach and rehabilitate the street kids of Ipswich.**

More descriptive reporting of carefully observed details, to introduce other characters but also to provide a brief respite from the high tension which has been building. The new characters are alarmed and alerted born-again Christians. They are providing free tea and coffee. They have a double-decker bus. And they have a long-range project to rehabilitate street kids in Ipswich. That's a lot of information packed into less than forty words.

> **The kid who punched the stranger could not understand why
> his friend was upset with him.**

> **"Man, I was angry!' he shouted, lacing his language with the
> usual obscenities. "You know how I get when I'm angry! I
> just have to take it out on someone!"**

The kid who punched the window wasn't buying it. He continued to rage at his friend, and he paced up and down the footpath in Bell St next to the bus.

He sat down next to the four people on the window ledge, still quaking with rage, still swearing at his friend who had punched the stranger, still expressing amazement that his friend would "deck" a stranger, still exhibiting shock and dismay that the stranger was bleeding.

His friend was also bleeding. He had busted a knuckle wide open and blood was running down his right middle finger, dripping onto his clothes and the pavement. His right hand was swelling rapidly. He was having trouble closing it. He walked up Bell St to get away from his friend's abuse.

Back to the kids, back to the tension, back to the conflict. More careful observation and detailed description. This time, however, the journalist confines the direct quotation to the inoffensive part and just tells the reader that the kid used the usual obscenities. The argument and the agitation are conveyed through paraphrase and description. The writer describes the kid's injury in detail, again using slang. Enter the Christians again, but the attention remains on the kid.

A couple of the Christians tried to pacify the kid who punched the window, but he would not be pacified. He continued to swear loudly.

Suddenly he swung his elbow and banged it hard against the window. Again the glass bowed ominously. Again it did not break.

This time a solidly built man, bearded and dressed in a black leather jacket and tattered blue jeans, tapped him on the shoulder and invited him to come away from the bus.

The kid thought they were going to fight, and that was okay with him. He was ready to release his rage and tension in a fight, even a fight he must surely lose to this tattooed man who is known on the street as Kelvin.

More vivid, up-close description, word pictures that show the reader the scene. When this new character enters, the journalist describes him in great detail: solid, bearded, black leather jacket, tattered jeans, tattoos. The kid's expecting a fight, probably because the man fits the stereotype of a thug. The reader may share the kid's interpretation, though the writer's description of the man is strictly objective.

The two of them walked down Bell St toward Brisbane St and stood nose to nose, talking and gesturing.

They walk away from the journalist. They are nose to nose and talking. We don't know what they are saying because they are too far away, but we can make out some gestures. Are they about to fight? The street names orient local readers. In cinematic terms, the word picture has changed from a close-up to a wide-angle distance shot.

Fifteen minutes later they returned to the bus, the kid calm, Kelvin's arm around his shoulder.

A temporary victory for the Christians, a small battle in their war to save the street kids of Ipswich.

They've returned to the bus, where we are. We weren't up the street with them, so we don't know from observation how Kelvin calmed the kid down. All we know from observation is that the kid is calm and they're friendly with one another. And we don't wait for details, for the story spirals us away to another block.

WHO ARE THESE PEOPLE?

If description and direct quotation give people breadth in your story, fleshing in their backgrounds gives them depth. People don't just come to life in your story. They existed long before you decided to write about them. They have backgrounds that help explain how they came to be where they are today. These explanations are important to help your reader understand the people you write about. So always make sure you sketch in some background information about the main people in your stories. Along with description, weave in such background information as education, training, qualifications, previous jobs and other life experiences. Such information goes a long way in making your characters three-dimensional. Here are some examples from the street kid series. They appear here as isolated paragraphs but in the stories the paragraphs were spiraled.

He may be a brand new person since accepting Jesus into his life, but before that he was where the street kids are now.

"I know where they're at," he said in an interview on the second storey of his bus. "I was into drugs and the lifestyle that goes with that for 10 years."

A 16-year-old brunette, stone cold sober, sits on Ramsey's bus. Eyes downcast, she pastes religious stickers in her Bible and tells you in her soft sing-songy voice that she ran away from home when she was 14.

And Kalamafoni, 34, a Tongan who says his only qualifications for his job are the 16 years he's put into it, emphasises that when he says he sees three kids a day, he means he says he sees three new kids a day, three kids he has not seen previously.

Another of the Ramsey team's recruits is Kelvin, a 35-year-old former biker.

The arrest was made by Constable 1/c Jim Madden, who was in plain clothes because he was relatively new to the district and not likely to be recognised out of uniform.

He said he could remember walking into parks in his youth and seeing dozens of family picnics in progress. Now, he said, you were lucky to see a few families picnicking in the park.

In each case, the background information helps the reader understand something about the person written about. The first person was into drugs for a decade, the second ran away from home at 14, the third has done his kind of work for 16 years, the fourth is a 35-year-old former biker, the fifth is new to the district and the sixth deplores the decline of family activities. Such small details help make them real, living, three-dimensional human beings, not cardboard cutouts that just pop up and speak in your story.

WRITE IN A BURST, REVISE AT LEISURE

As suggested in the previous chapter, write your first draft in one long creative burst. Once you have the first draft done, of course, you are not finished. You will rewrite your story at least once, possibly twice or even more times. So set it aside at least overnight or, even better, for a couple of days. The idea is to distance yourself from it so that when you come back to it, the logical side of your brain will bring a measure of objectivity to it. When you wrote it, your creative side wove into it an emotional attachment that was vital in the creation stage. But in the revision stage this emotional attachment will be an impediment. Now you need to look at the story as if you had never seen it before, as if you were your worst critic. In revising you need to apply cold, impersonal logic to your story without losing the warmth of its emotional fabric.

Revising your story takes a while, because if you do it properly, it takes several steps. Read it carefully. Expect to find that superfluous prepositional phrases, adjectives and adverbs crept into your story. They clog the sentences and obscure the meaning you intended. So on this first reading, remove such words without making any other changes to the text. If you are like most writers, this step alone should allow you to cut the story 10 to 15 per cent. Go through it again to correct any spelling, grammatical or style errors. Then read it again for content, to ensure it makes sense. Start to revise in earnest. You may reorganise the story; rewrite it; add, rearrange or delete paragraphs; change sentences around or delete them. Be ruthless. Sacrifice anything for clarity and liveliness. Then read the story word by word. Challenge every verb to make sure it is the liveliest you can use. Make sure every word is used correctly, every word is the right word, the best word.

When you are satisfied that you have done the best you can, you have finished your feature story and are ready to start on the next one.

Chapter 6
PUTTING IT ALL TOGETHER

$\mathbf{S}$o far you have studied the several components of feature writing in a disconnected way. In separate chapters you have looked at coming up with a workable idea, reporting and interviewing, writing a good lead using suspended interest, using transitions, quotations, anecdotes, description and other devices in the body and writing circular endings. It would be helpful at this point to analyse a published feature story so you can see how it all comes together in the finished product. Of course the best way to learn how to write feature stories is to write them and have them criticised by someone who can help you improve. But analysing feature stories in newspapers to pick up tips from professionals can be helpful.

For this analysis I have selected the third article in the highly commended eight-part Street Kid series published by the *Queensland Times*. The story is difficult to categorise because it falls between a personality profile and a news feature and contains elements of both. The main subject was a national celebrity particularly well-known in Ipswich. Hence, the story needed little personal description. The subject matter was deadly serious — socially unacceptable behaviour and redemption — yet could still be written in an informal and chatty manner. The story is a particularly good one for this exercise because in addition to providing good examples of many of the principles you have encountered in previous chapters, it also contains several mistakes that stemmed from failure to apply important principles.

Here is the story:

(1) When Pastor Jeff Ramsey talks to you in his quiet, reasonable voice, confidence and sincerity flash from his penetrating pale blue eyes.

(2) The Church of Christ pastor goes about the Lord's business with a firm conviction that God directs his activities.

(3) Ramsey's track record is excellent: He is the man who conducted the fund-raising campaign to send baby Paul McKee to America for his liver transplant operation.

(4) Now he is leading a tiny band of born-again Christian volunteers who have dedicated themselves to saving the street kids of Ipswich.

(5) Twenty street kids and about 20 "straight" people showed up at the boys' shelter on a chilly Wednesday night for a barbecue followed by a prayer meeting complete with religious songs, Bible studies, preaching and testimony about the Lord's intervention in people's lives.

(6) Ramsey, 36, who was leaving for Europe a few days later to attend two conferences on evangelism, was the centre of attention.

(7) After the singing and the testimony from other people Ramsey stood in the centre of the large lounge room, conducted a Bible study on the Gospel according to St Mark, then, still clutching his Bible, told the 50 people who sat in a circle against the walls about his 10 years as a drunkard, drug user and jailbird.

(8) And about how all that changed 10 years ago when he accepted Jesus into his life and gave his life to the Lord.

(9) As Ramsey spoke his wife Peta, 35, sat silently in a chair behind him, cuddling their sleepy younger daughter in her lap. Peta's eyes glistened as she listened to her husband recall their bad times and describe his redemption.

(10) "Before I became a Christian, I was involved with drugs and alcohol," Pastor Ramsey told his flock. "I'd been in jail."

(11) He said he frequently woke up unable to remember what had happened the night before.

(12) For years he was a drifter.

(13) "I've had more jobs than I've had breakfasts," he said. "I've had my own business and at one stage I was earning well over $1,000 a week."

(14) He was arrested for many of the offences common among people in the lifestyle he was leading.

(15) "I can remember being locked up for drunk and disorderly and obscene language and resisting arrest and all sorts of things," he said. "I've been in the lock-up so many times I couldn't even count them."

(16) Ramsey's delivery to his beloved flock was in the animated style of the witty and charismatic preacher he is, in contrast to the wary and tentative delivery of the same information to a stranger from the *Queensland Times* in initial interviews in March.

(17) Christian volunteers staff a bus in Bell St on Thursday nights.

(18) One March night in that bus he and Peta had discussed, separately, their life in the bike and drug scene and how they finally broke away from it.

(19) She said they had tried several times without success to break out of the drug scene.

(20) He said he habitually took amphetamines and LSD, smoked marijuana, ate hallucinogenic mushrooms and drank a lot of alcohol.

(21) "I'd get drunk and Peta and I would get on the motorcycle and go for rides on dark roads — 120, 130 kmh," he said.

(22) "One night a kangaroo jumped out right beside the bike as we went past. Another split second and we would have been killed. So we're lucky to be alive."

(23) Their life changed because his brother became a Christian.

(24) "I was just so stunned and fascinated by this change that had come over him, that I went to have a talk with him," Ramsey told the meeting.

(25) That talk led to many more, and after a great deal of prayer, meditation, soul-searching and personal challenges to God to prove Himself through signs that Ramsey could recognise, Ramsey became a Christian.

(26) Ever the pastor, he turns those laser eyes on you and tells you what it's like to be a Christian.

(27) "When you become a Christian, you become a brand new person," he said on the bus in March.

(28) "The spirit of the Lord came into me and transformed me utterly and absolutely. I threw away my cigarettes. I gave up alcohol and drugs.

(29) "I had my last drug two or three months after I got married, which was about three months before I became a Christian."

(30) Ramsey's conversion prompted Peta to convert.

(31) "I had always believed in God, but what made me dedicate my life to the Lord was the change in Jeff," she said.

(32) "He gave up drugs, alcohol, cigarettes from the first day. I knew that anything that could do that to him had to be real. It showed me that God was real."

(33) Later that night on the bus Ramsey explained how his turbulent lifestyle in the drug scene helped him now in his ministry on the streets of Ipswich.

(34) "It helps me to identify with these kids," he said. "I know where they're at."

(35) The kids appreciate that.

(36) "It's no use having a pastor who's grown up in a religious atmosphere," a 15-year-old street kid said. "His street ministry is going so well because he's done it all and he knows what we're doing."

(37) Ramsey said that despite their bizarre behaviour, what the kids are doing is not that unusual.

(38) "They're looking for what everyone is looking for — peace and security," he said that first night on the bus. "People look for those things in drugs, business, food, drink, money. But that's not where it's found.

(39) "I know from experience that even if you think you've found peace and security, it doesn't last long. It comes from God."

(40) The problem, he said, is that people have turned away from God.

(41) "There's an emptiness that won't be filled until people come home to God," he said.

(42) One of the street kids who came home to God is another 15-year-old blonde, a friend of the pregnant girl.

(43) The two of them went along to Ramsey's church one Sunday.

(44) "I just thought Christianity was Christianity, it was a lot of, um, well, crap," she said at the prayer meeting.

(45) "We went to church for a laugh. And I ended up peaking out to the max. I'm sitting there oh! wow! man, what's happening?! We ran out.

(46) "And I became a Christian sitting on a sewerage pipe."

(47) Another of the Ramsey team's recruits is Kelvin, a 35-year-old former biker.

(48) "When I became a Christian it felt like someone had cleaned the insides of me out with a wire brush and got rid of all the crud and all the scunginess," Kelvin said.

(49) Ramsey says he follows a pattern in doing the Lord's work.

(50) "There are two questions I always ask people: Do you know peace? Are you secure?" he said.

(51) "Nobody can answer yes to those questions unless they've met with God."

(52) Ramsey is aware that his views put him out of step with other people.

(53) "People might think I'm strange, but that's their prerogative to think that," he said.

(54) "I'm like the man who's won the million dollar lottery and he's got the cheque in his hand. He tells his friends he's won and they don't believe him.

(55) "But it doesn't matter whether they believe him or not. He has the cheque.

(56) "I'm like that man. I have the million-dollar cheque."

(57) Hence the confidence and the sincerity in his eyes.

Here is the analysis:

(1) Answer the frame question: What is going on here that is entertaining or interesting? The answer is Pastor Jeff Ramsey's confidence, dedication and strength of purpose. Note that only part of the focus for this story is set in the 22 words of the first paragraph, as the writer has opted for suspended interest by withholding what Ramsey will talk about. Identifying him as a pastor provides the clue that the story will concern religion and addressing the reader directly as "you" indicates it will be written informally. Ramsey was a celebrity, and his picture ran with this story, so it wasn't necessary to describe him much. But the photo could not portray his penetrating pale [note the alliteration] blue eyes, so they are described. Note the strength of "flash". He has penetrating pale blue eyes that flash. All that description is fairly objective. The description of his voice as quiet and reasonable is less objective but not overly subjective, since most people would likely agree on the meaning of those two adjectives when applied to a speaking style. The thrust of the lead is that this confident man has something sincere to say and is worth listening to.

(2) Repeating "pastor" is the transition. Naming his sect is part of his identification. You should expect some documentation later in the story of the assertion that he is convinced God directs his activities.

(3) Repeating "Ramsey" is the transition. This paragraph reminds Ipswich readers that they know Ramsey. He became a national celebrity when he led the drive in which the community raised enough money to send the baby to America for a life-saving operation not available in Australia at that time. The paragraph also establishes, through unobtrusive backgrounding, Ramsey's credibility in this story as a caring person.

(4) "Now" is the transition. This paragraph brings the reader up to date on what Ramsey's doing now. It contains the added background information that he is a born-again Christian and that he is leading volunteers in an effort to save street kids in Ipswich. And it ends the suspended interest by specifying that the focus of this story will be Ramsey working with street kids. This is the end of a block.

(5) Repeating "street kids" is the transition to the new block. The paragraph is a transition that takes the reader from the focus-setting block to a block that starts the story proper. A peak of suspense is created. Factual information is provided on the number of people, about evenly divided between street kids and others. The word "straight" may not be the best word to describe the others, since one of its meanings is "not gay", but in the context of providing contrast to street kids, it probably works. More factual information: it's taking place at the boys' shelter [not further described in this story but mentioned at length in one of the previous stories in the series], it's a chilly Wednesday night and there's a barbecue — a common Aussie event that readers can identify with. More factual information about a prayer meeting that people can identify with either from their own experience or from motion pictures and television — religious songs, Bible studies, preaching and testifying. The born-again aspect of their faith is reflected in the belief that the Lord intervenes in people's lives. This could have been made clearer and more specific if it had read: the Lord's *direct* intervention in people's *daily* lives. Not only would that have made the connection better in this paragraph, it would have provided better documentation for the assertion in paragraph (2) that Ramsey is convinced the Lord directs his activities.

(6) Using "Ramsey" is the transition, and the sentence provides a little background about him — his age and the fact that he's off to Europe to learn more about his life's work — evangelism — and documentation for his leadership — he's the centre of attention. The peak of suspense continues.

(7) "After" is the transition. This is deliberately a very long sentence — 56 words — painting a word picture through a lot of description and up-close detail and

providing a mood shift in the story. The first part shows the passage of time —
Ramsey relinquished the attention of attention to others, it's after the barbecue,
they've sung their songs and other people have testified about their religious
experiences. Now it's Ramsey's turn. He's reacquired the centre of attention and is
standing in the middle of a large room, documented by the fact that 50 people are
sitting around the walls. He's conducted a Bible study based on the Gospel of St
Mark. He's still clutching his Bible. Then comes the reason for the mood shift, the
information that comes at the end for its shock value. He talks about his 10 years as
a drunkard, drug user and jailbird. The writer intended the long sentence to lull
readers into a placid rhythm then jar the mood with the information about the pastor's
unsavoury past. The peak continues.

(8) "And" provides the transition. This paragraph started out as the last clause in
the previous sentence. But the writer decided the jolt in (7) would be more effective
if the sentence ended with the unsavoury information, thus pulling the reader up
with a sharp shock. By following the very long sentence with a short one about
accepting Jesus, the writer again changed the mood, suddenly relieving the shock
with information that put the unsavoury information well into the past and that told
the reader what changed Ramsey from a no-hoper to a widely respected man of the
cloth. In other words, the writer provided a valley of resolution after building
suspense for three paragraphs.

(9) "As Ramsey spoke" is the transition. The reader is invited to take a breath and
digest the information contained in (7) and (8) with a shift of attention away from
Ramsey to a word picture of his wife Peta. The observations are all objective: she's
sitting quietly behind him, cuddling their younger daughter. She's calm but her
eyes glisten. Then the attention shifts back to Ramsey as he tells a room full of
people about their bad times and his redemption, creating a peak of suspense. It sets
up the first direct quotation of the story. From a practical standpoint, it was necessary
to introduce his wife into the story, and this was the first logical place to do that. It
works because it interposes a familiar domestic scene between the pastor's
paraphrased revelations and his quoted remarks.

(10) The quotation follows on from the set-up and begins the anecdotes through
which the reader will learn about Ramsey's earlier life. He said he was involved
with drugs and alcohol and had been in jail. That documents paragraphs (7), (8) and
(9) by putting the assertions in his own words. And it reminds the reader that this is
being said in public by mentioning the flock. It provides a valley of resolution.

(11, 12) "He" is the transition. Both paragraphs summarise and paraphrase things that Ramsey said about his former life and set up the quotation in the next paragraph. A peak of suspense is created. Note the writer is careful to attribute to Ramsey by using "said" in (11). That attribution carries over into (12).

(13) The direct quotation follows on from the set-up in (12), and provides a valley of resolution in the punchline. But (11) has not been documented, which is a flaw. The second sentence of the direct quotation is obscure. It is vague and unconnected. This is also a flaw in the story. That sentence does not belong in this story at all. All it does is interrupt the flow.

(14) A transition paragraph setting up direct quotations and providing a peak of suspense by introducing an anecdote and leaving it for the source to finish.

(15) More anecdote in a punchline in his own words about his unsavoury past, providing a valley of resolution.

(16) "Ramsey" is the transition that links the present block into a complex transition requiring three paragraphs to get to a new block. It starts out with a mixture of objective [animated style] and somewhat subjective [witty and charismatic] description of the prayer meeting. Then it contrasts the scene in this block with Ramsey's wary and tentative delivery months ago in an interview with the reporter. The purpose of the transition is to shift the story to a new block, to take the reader back in time for things that were said in the past. The writer is playing fair with the reader by making the context clear. A peak of suspense is created by raising the contrast without explaining it.

(17) There is no transition. There is no indication that the initial interviews in March from (16) had anything to do with Christian volunteers, a bus, Bell St or Thursday nights. The paragraph contributes nothing and, which is worse, it interrupts the flow. With proper transition, the background information about the bus in Bell St on Thursday nights would have made sense because it would have reminded local readers about the bus they might have seen during late-night shopping excursions.

(18) "One March night" is the proper transition from (16), making it painfully obvious that (17) should not have been in the story. The paragraph completes the transition in time from the lounge room back to the bus in March. As well, it indicates that during separate interviews, the Ramseys discussed some of the topics that Ramsey told the flock. The new block begins on a peak of suspense about their travails.

(19) "She" is the transition. The paragraph touches lightly through paraphrase some of what she said without resolving the suspense.

(20) "He" is the transition. The transition back to March allowed the writer to specify which drugs Ramsey had generalised about in the passages quoted from the prayer meeting. The revelations are made in a matter-of-fact delivery that cries out for more detail. The writer could not use the direct quotations and give the punchline to the source because the direct quote ended with a drug. So the writer paraphrased the quote to end his sentence with "alcohol" to provide a set-up for the following paragraphs' quotes in which Ramsey provides anecdotes about their previous life.

(21, 22) The quotes follow on from the set-up and provide anecdotes that contain specific details in his own words of generalisations they both had made about their perilous life in the bike and drug scene and the need to break away from that life. The quotes are colourful.

(23) "Their life" is the transition, and the sentence introduces a new block dealing with Ramsey's redemption. It sets up a direct quotation and creates a peak of suspense by raising the question of how the brother's conversion was involved.

(24) The quotation is the punchline for the anecdote and follows on from the set-up by beginning the explanation of how his brother's conversion led to his own. But it does not resolve the suspense. Also, the attribution moves the reader forward in time to the prayer meeting. Again, the writer makes sure the reader knows the context of the situation. So far the reader has moved from the prayer meeting, to the bus, then back to the meeting.

(25) "That talk" is the transition. The writer again paraphrased Ramsey to get quickly to the point of his becoming a Christian and resolving the suspense. The direct quotes did not lend themselves to the story.

(26) "Ever the pastor" is the transition. The story has reached a critical point. Ramsey is about to talk to us in that quiet, reasonable voice, exuding confidence and sincerity. The writer wishes to evoke the memory from the lead and does it by coming back to "those laser eyes". He sets up a direct quotation and creates a peak of suspense.

(27) "When you become a Christian" provides the transition, and the quotation follows on from the set-up and continues the suspense. It is a proper punchline for the set-up. As well, the reader is whisked back to the bus, for that is where Ramsey made that statement. Another time shift, but the reader is able to keep up with it because the writer takes the time to make the context clear.

(28, 29) The poignant direct quotations relate anecdotes that document Ramsey's conversion to Christianity, document his conviction that God directly intervenes in his life, resolve the suspense and end a block.

(30) "Ramsey's conversion" is the transition, and the sentence itself is a transition to a new block about his wife's conversion and creates a peak of suspense. It also introduces her as the next speaker.

(31, 32) Her direct quotations provide the punchline to the anecdote, relate some anecdotes of her own, document the writer's exposition about her conversion and create a valley of resolution. Note the attribution "she said" in (31) reminds the reader that the speaker is no longer Ramsey but his wife.

(33) "Later" is the transition, and the writer reminds the reader that we're still at the bus. Attention shifts back to Ramsey and the exposition introduces a new block about how his past helps Ramsey in the present, creating a peak of suspense.

(34) The direct quotation is a punchline and follows on from the set-up and furthers the new block by continuing the peak of suspense: Where are they at?

(35) These four words provide transition to a new speaker. The suspense still has not been resolved.

(36) A direct quotation that follows on from the set-up, creates a valley of resolution and finishes the block.

(37) "Ramsey" brings the attention back to the main subject and the exposition announces a new block. Notice the alliteration in bizarre behaviour. A peak of suspense is created: Why isn't it unusual?

(38, 39) The direct quotations resolve the suspense by relating street kid behaviour to everyone's search for peace and security as normal activities and sets up a new peak of suspense by putting its achievement in doubt.

(40) The sentence is a transition to a new block and sets up a peak of suspense by stating a problem. Notice the writer broke a rule about not breaking into a sentence early with attribution. That was done for emphasis and effect.

(41) The direct quotation resolves the suspense.

(42) "Came home to God" provides transition to a new speaker and starts a new block. The paragraph is sloppy. The street kid is described as "another" blonde and as "a friend of the pregnant girl". But she is the first blonde to appear in the story

and no pregnant girl has appeared. The mistakes arose because paragraph (36) as originally written identified that 15-year-old as a pregnant blonde. In that context, paragraph (42) makes perfect sense. But the writer decided that the pregnancy in (36) was irrelevant and deleted the reference to a pregnant blonde. Then he neglected to make the necessary follow-on changes in (42). The error points up two things to remember. First, sub-editing usually has a ripple effect in a story; when you make changes, be sure to change all other affected mentions. Second, this is precisely the kind of error that block writing is supposed to eliminate; there should be no reference in a subsequent block (42) to a peripheral source whose minor contribution to the story took place in a previous block (36).

(43) "The two of them" is the transition. The sentence continues the peak of suspense by introducing in exposition an anecdote of how she came home to God.

(44) Using her direct quote shows off her colourful way of expressing herself. The paragraph also alerts the reader to a time shift back to the prayer meeting and continues the suspense.

(45, 46) In the punchline to the anecdote, her direct quotations again exhibit her youthful enthusiasm and use of slang. Note the use of exclamation points within the direct quotations to indicate her emphasis. Her punchline is a beauty.

(47) "Another" is the transition to a new block and a new speaker.

(48) His direct quotation is the punchline of his anecdote. His striking metaphor and language add his experience to the blonde's about becoming a Christian. Both help document Ramsey's earlier statement about becoming a new person when you become a Christian, way back in paragraph (27). That's a violation of the block writing rule. But the writer felt putting the blonde and the biker after (27), would break up the block dedicated to Ramsey's own conversion. So, knowing that he would eventually to use the colourful quotes of the two street kids, he constructed the block about people coming home to God.

(49) "Ramsey" is the transition to a new block. A peak of suspense is created: What's the pattern? The sentence also introduces him as the next speaker.

(50, 51) He explains the pattern in the punchline to resolve the suspense. The quotation illuminates the conviction of his faith.

(52) Another peak of suspense is raised: How does he handle the knowledge that he's out of step?

(53, 54, 55, 56) He's answering the question with a striking metaphor, so the writer stays well out of the way, letting the source explain the depth of his beliefs in his own way.

(57) "Hence" is the transition to a circular ending.

The knowledge you now possess about feature writing should stimulate you to read your newspaper differently. Where before you read for content, you should begin to read for technique and style. All good feature writers have techniques you can try out to improve your writing.

Chapter 7

COMPUTER-ASSISTED REPORTING

Computers have been in newspapers for more than a decade. Journalists use word-processing software packages on networked terminals to write stories and send them electronically to sub-editors, who do their work online and in turn send the stories to be electronically typeset. Each journalist has an individual queue on the main computer in which to store notes from stories-in-progress and other confidential information. An internal email system delivers your memo to a colleague's queue.

After starting out as a production tool, the computer has revolutionised journalism at both ends. At the receiving end, home computers enable people to access online news and entertainment from newspapers, magazines, wire services, and radio and television organisations that maintain websites on the Internet.

And at the producing end, desktop and laptop computers have changed how journalists go about reporting and writing feature stories. The journalistic principles remain unchanged, but the computer has unlocked a powerful set of information-gathering techniques known collectively as computer-assisted reporting (CAR). These are techniques that every journalist should have, doesn't have yet, but will have in the future.

WHAT IS CAR?

CAR is mainly, but not exclusively, a way of analysing public records. The three main uses of CAR are to generate story ideas, to research investigative feature stories, and to identify, locate and interview sources. CAR tools include email, Internet browsers and search engines, spreadsheets and databases. CAR does not replace the traditional techniques of reporting, but can be used in addition to them for better stories. The best CAR stories combine the power of number-crunching with in-depth interviews of those affected, to put the human face on the facts.

To take full advantage of these advances, journalists will have to learn mathematics and statistics and become more computer literate. Governments, political parties, corporations, even sports organisations make decisions based on computer analyses. Those in the know tell journalists only what they want to reveal, and journalists write their stories from this spoon-fed information. Brant Houston, executive director of Investigative Reporters and Editors, likens this process to feeding time at the zoo, with the journalists waiting in cages to be fed pellets of information by their keepers, their sources. To be independent of those who would manipulate them, journalists must equip themselves to crunch the numbers themselves.

CAR requires a computer loaded with word-processing, spreadsheet and database software packages and, ideally though not absolutely required, a Web browser and access to the Internet. Some universities provide all this in networked computer labs. To get online from home, you need a computer, a modem to connect you to a telephone line, a communication program and an access provider to reach the Internet.

It is beyond the scope of this book to teach you how to use all of these tools. Rather, the purpose here is to make you aware of what they do and when journalists use them. So the discussions below presuppose that you know how to use, for example, a spreadsheet or a Web browser, and mainly focus on their journalistic applications. The aim is to alert you to techniques that will enable you to produce richer, deeper and more meaningful feature stories, some utilising worldwide sources hitherto unavailable to you.

If they're not connected from work, journalists should be among the hundreds of thousands of Australians who daily go online from home through one of hundreds of Internet Service Providers (ISPs). ISPs provide software programs that put you through their gateways to the Internet and allow you to perform tasks there. On the Internet, customers can access email, databases on almost any subject, news services such as the ABC and CNN, Australian and foreign newspapers, radio stations, live concerts, football matches, chats with celebrities, hit audio and video clips complete with lyrics for singing along, thousands of newsgroups where people discuss through email their shared interests, hard-core pornography, and online shopping malls.

ISPs charge for time spent online using email or browsing the Internet. You dial in from your computer and get attached to an ISP computer connected to the Internet. Some ISPs charge by the hour and others charge a set monthly fee with a certain number of free hours before another charge kicks in. Some of the larger Australian ISPs are Ozemail, Powerup, Global Info-Links, Access One and Telstra's Big Pond. Prices and services vary, and there have been complaints about some ISPs not making good on promised services, so it pays to shop around. The giant American ISPs, CompuServe and America Online, offer Australian customers the hundreds of research, shopping and news, entertainment and information services available in their home country.

THE RISE OF CAR

After John Howard was elected Prime Minister in March 1996, news leaked that he would appoint Ian McLachlan his Minister for Defence. This rumor prompted a Labor politician to quip derisively that McLachlan, a former National Farmers' Federation President, had never had a defence thought in his life. After Mr Howard named his Cabinet, Peter Charlton, then the political editor of Brisbane's *Courier-Mail*, included this paragraph in his feature story analysing the appointments:

> **Ian McLachlan as Defence Minister is an interesting choice. A quick search of the parliamentary data base last night showed the words "McLachlan" and "defence" in a speech occurred just once in the six years the gentleman-farmer has been in Parliament.**

Charlton was able to verify that McLachlan had had at least that one defence thought because he had used a CAR tool to find a scrap of information in one McLachlan speech in "the parliamentary data base" — a computerised version of the full text of every speech made by every MP.

This was a significant shift in reporting technique. Charlton was not prompted by the Labor politician's quip to get a rejoinder from a Coalition spokesperson, in the tradition of the journalistic charge/denial format. Instead, acting on the quip, he used a computer to dig out the facts from a database, then *on his own authority* analysed McLachlan's appointment as "interesting", a wry euphemism for "puzzling" in view of the new Minister's previous lack of interest in defence. Charlton's story did not depend on two spin doctors scoring political points off each other by spoon-feeding him pellets of self-serving information.

The Charlton example may strike you as trivial, but its very simplicity crystallises the revolution. Since 1988, stories using CAR have won Pulitzer Prizes in the United States. These were all complex investigative journalistic enterprises.

Journalists who can use a computer to gather raw data, analyse the figures or trends and draw conclusions, can uncover angles those in charge might wish to play down or ignore. This means that instead of being at the mercy of self-serving sources for information and interpretation, journalists can develop original investigative feature stories. US newspapers routinely send their journalists to week-long CAR training sessions. The National Institute of Computer-assisted Reporting has trained thousands of American journalists over the past few years.

Professor John T. (Tom) Johnson of San Francisco State University has been in the forefront of CAR education and training for several years. He agrees with researchers who classify individual journalists within newsrooms as "A-team" or "B-Team", as newspapers are designated — with "A" newspapers being what Aussies call the quality press. These newspapers display "a richer vision of the complex issues of the community, nation and world, and they are willing or able to devote resources to reporting them". As well, they tend to cover the issues in depth and value imagination on the part of their reporters. The "B" newspapers are all the rest. They scratch the surface of the news and lean toward sensationalistic coverage.

Johnson says that "A" journalists "are brighter and more intellectually aggressive". They don't wait for assignments but inundate their chiefs of staff with story ideas. They understand that a complex story's context goes back in time past the clippings in the library and reaches ahead farther than today's deadline. They enjoy the challenges of complex stories and have reasonable expertise that goes beyond the skills requirements of the job — perhaps in statistics, accounting, psychology, history or law.

By contrast, Johnson calls "B" reporters pedestrian in their approach to stories and secure in their status quo. They depend on others to guide them in their daily tasks, asking who to call for information and afterwards checking back for more guidance on how to proceed. They also seek help during the writing stage. Johnson said that every news organisation needs "B" journalists to handle the routine stories, but "A" newspapers must also have some "A" journalists. CAR, with its ability to uncover complex investigative stories, is the perfect vehicle for "A" journalists.

CAR IN AUSTRALIA

Australian journalists have been slow to take up CAR, just as Australian newspapers were well behind American newspapers and, indeed, behind their own readers, in going online. Newspaper executives woke up to the Internet when they realised that ordinary Australians in ever-increasing numbers were using their home computers to find fresher news than was appearing in their newspapers. Much online news is updated every hour. By contrast, most news in morning newspapers is at least nine hours old and foreign news can be 24 hours old.

Going online has changed the lives of some ordinary Australians. Jo Oliphant, who writes the "Lost in Cyberspace" column in Brisbane's *Courier-Mail*, emailed me a telling example. Oliphant, who admitted that she was terrified of computers until she was persuaded to become the newspaper's online reporter and columnist, conducted an interview by email with a grazier's wife who credited the Internet with transforming her life by reducing the isolation she feels living west of Longreach. She uses the Internet to check stock and weather information and to make direct submissions on policies important to her, policies she can read in full for herself on a government website rather than a truncated version in a newspaper.

In addition to scooping their own newspapers, Australians could get information online that newspapers were not providing. They were tapping into the more than 10,000 online groups devoted to discussing subjects they were interested in, such as Greenpeace, rock bands, kinky sex, *X-files* plots, cocker spaniels, dirty jokes, computer games.

Editors realised that they had better start covering this communication phenomenon, so they assigned journalists to cover the Internet as a round. From there it's only a short leap for a journalist to use CAR techniques. But while CAR was gaining a foothold among some Australian freelance journalists, it was not a leap that many newspaper journalists were making. University of Queensland journalism lecturer Kerry Green wrote in 1994 that CAR would catch on in Australia "probably sooner than later". But by late 1996, he had lost some of his optimism.

Most managers were reluctant to pay for intensive training in CAR techniques or for access to the Internet. Besides the expense, few newspapers were willing to release journalists from mundane tasks to give them time to attend training courses necessary to learn CAR. Deakin University journalism lecturer Stephen Quinn found that only two of the 50 Australian newspapers he surveyed had offered its journalists any kind of training in the deeper levels of CAR.

Quinn points out that basic CAR — email and Web browsing — is relatively easy to learn and journalists can turn out stories with it fairly quickly, whereas deeper CAR techniques to crunch the numbers in a massive government database require substantial training. Moreover, on the job, CAR projects can take scores of staff hours yet yield little publishable copy, so its public service value in uncovering major stories by analysing thousands of records embedded in official databases is not seen by managers as cost-effective. Even so, "A" newspapers ought to have "A" journalists capable of doing complex CAR stories, and even "B" journalists can learn basic CAR for simpler stories under some guidance, though most managers seem unlikely to spend the money.

But just as Luddite journalists in the 1980s swore they'd never give up their trusty typewriters for computers, those who resist CAR are fighting a losing battle. Make no mistake about it, CAR is here to stay. As US journalism educator Robin Lind scolds: "Shame on you if you don't use the tools that are available in your generation". To my way of thinking, CAR should be in every journalist's toolkit alongside telephone books, interviewing techniques, property searches, covering the courts.

Since CAR skills cannot be learnt on the job in Australia, journalism lecturers have taken the lead by teaching it in their universities. Since the number of jobs in the industry is fewer than the number of graduates produced each year, teaching CAR was a way of putting their students on the cutting edge to increase their employability.

Beyond the transformation in journalism, CAR should help enhance the democratic process in Australia by combatting government secrecy. Whereas in the United States it is assumed that the vast majority of government information should be made easily available to the public, Australian governments withhold information from public scrutiny. They commonly give such excuses as Cabinet solidarity, protection of privacy or protection of commercial advantage. Often the real reason governments withhold information is to save embarrassing the government by exposing incompetence.

In highlighting a barrier to CAR gaining an early foothold in Australia, QUT Journalism lecturer Suellen Tapsall compared and contrasted the handling of information about food hygiene problems in restaurants in Brisbane and in Detroit. The Brisbane City Council in July 1996 announced that more than a third of 3,300 city food outlets posed a high or medium risk to customers because of unhealthy food-handling processes. The Council refused to name the outlets involved, refused to say what kinds of outlets they were, and refused to give their general locations. Meanwhile, a Detroit television station was running a list of the city's dirtiest dozen restaurants, based on a computer analysis of health inspection reports, a service much appreciated by members of the public, if not by the restaurants. Sadly, as a footnote to the comparison, Tapsall reported that senior Australian journalists later agreed that the Council should have withheld the information so as not to harm the restaurant trade. A lapdog journalistic culture that accepts any official secrecy, but especially in a matter of public health, is despicable.

This obsequious culture should change as the next few generations of university journalism students take their place on newspapers. In the late 1990s journalism students — teenagers, most of them — have been producing as class assignments sophisticated and socially significant investigative feature stories that are beyond the capabilities of most experienced journalists. At job interviews they have been showing those stories to prospective employers. And upon taking up positions on Australia's newspapers, they have been pressing their employers for the time, the money and the equipment to continue to use CAR.

Australian journalism in the late 1990s, then, is on the cusp of an era in which using CAR will be as routine as using the telephone. And as more and more journalists harness the power of the computer to do stories in the public interest that governments and individuals with vested interests prefer not be done, they will make officials more accountable by putting them under public pressure to release more and more information in searchable databases.

DATABASES AND SPREADSHEETS

Commercial database services opened the door to CAR, according to Nora Paul, News Library Director of the Poynter Institute of Media Studies in St Petersburg, Florida. To demonstrate the increasing importance of such databases, she has charted the entries in Gale's Directory of Online Databases. In 1979, Gale's listed 221 producers and 300 databases. By 1990 it was 1,950 producers and 3,943 databases. And by 1995 the numbers had leaped to 2,202 producers and 5,342 databases. Databases can be analysed with two powerful tools — database managers and spreadsheets. Using either tool, you can sort and group data for at-a-glance analysis. Since spreadsheets perform dozens of mathematical, financial and statistical computations, they are invaluable for analysing such items as budgets, crime rates, balance sheets, highway black spots, health and safety inspections, length of jail sentences, auto registrations.

Lorenz and Vivian described several CAR projects carried out by US journalists: one in Houston created and maintained a homicide database using police reports; another traced political donations from contributors to candidates using information required by law to be published; another analysed the race of people given traffic tickets by local police and verified a rumor that Afro-Americans were more likely to be ticketed than whites; another looked through seven million financial transactions in his state's general fund to generate stories about questionable connections between members of the legislature and companies doing business with the state. What makes such stories journalistically sound is the quality of the information that reaches the audience. It comes from analysing official records.

Three CAR projects that have been done in several US locales are examination of bridge inspection reports to identify the most dangerous bridges in a state, analysis of dog registrations to determine which are the most popular names, and inspection of health inspection records to alert the public to a city's cleanest and dirtiest restaurants. Investigative Reporters and Editors and the National Institute of Computer Assisted Reporting stand ready to provide journalists from around the world with story ideas encompassing CAR projects and advice on how to carry them out.

The *Cincinnati Enquirer*'s projects reporter, Mark Braykovich, advised members of a discussion list not to think in terms of what would make a good CAR story. Instead, think what would make a good story, then see if CAR can help that story. If not, use only traditional reporting methods. If so, still use the traditional methods but add CAR to the mix. Braykovich sifts through databases looking for stories because, he says, almost any database has some sort of story in it.

Databases are produced by such sources as government agencies, newspapers, magazines, professional and education associations and dissident, protest and activist groups. Commercial database services store the information on computers and on-sell access to their customers. University libraries are major customers of commercial database services, so staff and students can search databases of bibliographies and abstracts; articles and transcripts; books and directories; government documents and public records. Journalism students who learn to use such databases for academic essays can easily think ways of using them for feature stories, such as in gathering background for a story-in-progress. Consulting with librarians is a good way to learn which databases are available to you and what sort of information you'll find in them. Feature writers can make use of all kinds of databases.

Databases are stored on computers, on CD-ROMs, and on the World Wide Web. A computerised full-text database treats every major word as if it were an index item. Excluded are common words like "a", "an", "the", "but", "with", "or", "on", "in". But aside from such exceptions, you can ask a database to locate any word you consider important to your research. You type in a "keyword", and the computer software takes you to every place in the text where that word occurs. A Boolean search enables you to focus even more narrowly to find word combinations: A *and* B; A *or* B; A *not* B.

Such databases of text can be downloaded and imported into word-processing programs on PCs. An example would be every article in *The Age* between specified dates, on, say, whether Mark Taylor should have been replaced as Australian cricket captain during a bout of bad form. The stories could be searched one at a time with the word processor, or imported into a free-form database manager such as askSam, which is capable of Boolean searching all the articles in one continuous operation.

Databases containing numbers can be downloaded into spreadsheets and database managers. Despite a high level of secrecy, all levels of government in Australia release huge collections of statistics. Here are just a few examples of what you could find in a database: How many people live in Australia; how many were born here; how many came here from other countries and which other countries and when; how many couples got married and divorced; how many babies were born and the ages of their mothers; how many Australians are unemployed; how many are university students; what our average age is, our average income, our average level of education; how much beer we drink annually; how many and what kinds of crime were committed last year and where; how many houses and office buildings were built; how much money people lost in casinos; how many people abuse drugs and alcohol; how much coal and wool we export; how much wheat we grow; how many people are homeless; where we go for holidays; how much the price of petrol varies from locale to locale; how much the government receives in taxes; how much it spends and what it spends the money on. And we know every word every MP says in Parliament, which brings us back to Peter Charlton's search of the parliamentary database.

Charlton conducted a Boolean search of the database of Parliamentary speeches, asking for all instances in which "McLachlan" *and* "defence" appeared in the same speech. The computer searched every speech made in Parliament since McLachlan became an MP and replied that there had been only that one instance — one "hit", in the parlance of computerised database searches.

Such quick access to huge amounts of information is a revolutionary advance for any kind of researcher, but it is particularly valuable for journalists, who almost always conduct their research, even for feature stories, in a hurry. Of course, obtaining information is not the end of the process. It is only the beginning. Information is useful only if a journalist makes it meaningful to readers. Finding the McLachlan/ defence needle in the haystack of speeches enabled Charlton to make the one "hit" meaningful to his readers by independently confirming the Labor quip.

Freelance journalists were quick to tap into online databases. Elizabeth Walton, a freelancer who lives in rural New South Wales, does a lot of feature stories on the environment. She taps into databases maintained by such organisations as the

Environmental Resource and Education Network, Greenpeace, CSIRO, and the US Environmental Protection Agency. She says the World Wide Web is a good place to contact activist and reformist groups, information from which helps her balance the information she gets from Government, Opposition and minority party policies. The ability to download information quickly from such diverse sources gives her stories a richness that would be impossible to achieve with traditional methods of interviewing.

The usual journalistic caveat applies when researching on the Internet. As in life, do not believe everything you see and hear. You cannot trust all the information. It might be dead wrong. Anyone can put anything on the Internet, so be especially critical when researching. Woodbury and Schmitz suggest some questions you should ask yourself: "Who put the information there? What is their mission? What is their reputation? Do they have a potential conflict of interest? Are there careful reasons given for their claims?" In other words, you should approach databases with the same caution you would approach any source.

CREATING AND USING YOUR OWN DATABASES

You can design and create your own databases using a database program such as Microsoft Access or Novell's Quattro Pro, or a spreadsheet program such as Microsoft Excel, or their equivalent Mac program, FileMaker Pro. All spreadsheets have a built-in database function but have the added advantage of enabling the user to do sophisticated arithmetic, financial and statistical computations. Modern software includes wizards to help you create individualised databases to keep track of CDs, books, videos, household expenses, crime rates, arrest rates, birth rates, population shifts, interest rates and countless other personal and professional items of interest.

A little forethought goes a long way in creating a database, according to Mike Wendland, leader of Detroit television station WDIV's investigative reporting team and a CAR practitioner and trainer. Wendland gave the following advice to a CAR seminar in April 1995 at the Poynter Institute: Keep your database simple by including only those fields (columns) you're sure you'll need and keep it logical by setting it up in the same order that you'll be inputting the data. Take your time, allowing a couple of minutes for a half-dozen fields. Check for errors every five records (rows), and correct them immediately. Save your work every five minutes to protect yourself against a loss of data from a power surge or failure, and back up the whole file every hour.

As you sit at your computer, contemplating a huge number of records with dozens of fields, how do you find a story in all that data? Finding the story under those circumstances is not as easy as rewriting an official handout on what the government spokesperson says is the meaning of the data. Finding the story can be extremely intuitive. You have to "interview" the data. Wendland's advice is to sort the data alphabetically or numerically so you can scroll through it time and again looking for patterns, trends, recurring names, offences, locations, failures, successes. Your journalistic sense should uncover stories embedded in any database, including some records you do not even think of as databases.

Soon after journalists switched from typewriters to newsroom computers, they realised they could treat their transcribed notes and stories as full-text databases. They used keyword searches to call up direct quotes and previous stories for news and feature stories they were currently working on. Before computers, journalists had to retype information from clippings found in the newspaper's library. Computers enabled them to save time and effort. After importing the previous information into the present story, they would only have to rework it a little to freshen it and make it fit smoothly. These techniques were explained to me as part of my orientation in 1986 when I took a six-month leave from then-QIT to work as a senior journalist at the *Queensland Times* in Ipswich. I used them frequently to turn out features and later to write the first edition of this textbook.

At the *QT* I taped interviews and transcribed them and my hand-written notes into files stored in my confidential queue. When writing a story, I would open a window, then call up a quotes file. In another window, I would start writing a feature story. When I came to a point where I wanted to use a direct quote or insert some background information, I could quickly do a keyword search in the quotes window, locate appropriate copy and import it into the story window.

This CAR technique saved me enormous amounts of time and retyping. Some quotes appeared in more than one story, but I only typed the quotes once, when I was transcribing them off the tape recorder or out of my notebook. After that, the *QT* main computer kept them ever ready in my queue, and I could tell the computer to find them and insert them where I needed them.

Back at QIT, when I wrote *Newspaper Feature Writing*, I used the same techniques on my PC. In several years of teaching Feature Writing, I had provided students with a typed critique for each story. In the early 1980s, I had switched from a typewriter to a database program. That program printed a copy of the critique for the student and saved an electronic copy on my disk. Those critiques on my disk were a fully searchable, full-text database of common problems encountered by beginning feature writers. In writing this book, I addressed those problems. Keyword searching was much faster than reading through a decade of story critiques typed on paper.

Your contact book is a database

Besides notes and stories, journalists always have at hand their contact book, in which they keep the names and contact details of people they have interviewed or are likely to interview. In a typical contact book are people's names, titles, organisations, addresses, telephone and fax numbers, perhaps a note or two about them or their areas of expertise.

Traditionally, journalists keep this information alphabetically or by section in a spiral or loose-leaf notebook. The inconvenience of such a listing scheme is that you can only access it page by page. In other words, if you want to look up Joe Blogg's telephone number and exact title, you turn to the B listings and look him up. A book is fine for that kind of search and its advantage is that you can carry it around with you. But if you needed to find all sources with expertise in budget analysis, you'd have to look at almost every entry on almost every page and make notes. But since a contact book is a database, you can keep the information on a spreadsheet instead of in a book.

So your record, Joe Bloggs, might contain fields for all those categories listed two paragraphs above plus many more. The real advantage of a computerised contact book over one in a spiral notebook is that you can find information by querying in any field. You can quickly locate those starting with S, all those with expertise in budget analysis, all those with telephone numbers in Geelong, all the men, all the women, all those located in Western Australia, all those who mentioned the topic you're researching, all those who are married or single, all those whose identities you do not reveal, all those who prefer cricket to Aussie Rules. And Boolean searching will find all those who are located in Western Australia *and* have expertise in budget analysis. The ability to unleash the power of your computer outweighs the disadvantage of not being able to carry it around with you, for you can always print out the information you need for the story you're working on, and carry that report around with you.

Even more versatile for a contact book than a spreadsheet or a database manager is a personal information manager such as Microsoft Schedule or Lotus Organiser. These have wizards to help you create databases of your contacts. With these programs, you can look up a source's telephone number, click on it, and your computer will dial the number using its communication program and modem. As well as keeping your contact book, such an organiser also has an electronic diary that looks onscreen like the one you probably carry around with you. But the electronic one has an alarm you can set to remind you of appointments, it helps you keep a "to do" list with pop-up reminders a few days in advance, it has a built-in notebook, it has a year planner and it will keep track of your important dates.

USING THE INTERNET

The Internet is a computer network made up of thousands of computer networks. It was set up in the 1960s during the Cold War as a US Defence Department initiative. The idea was to house sensitive information simultaneously in many computers around the world. These computers communicated with one another through a sophisticated linkage system, so that if part of the system failed, the information would not be lost. The system was designed to survive nuclear holocaust. Users needed high-level security clearance. Messages took many routes to reach their destination, and if part of the system was shut down, say for maintenance, a message would find another path to its destination. Since the Internet is everywhere at once and nowhere in particular, it is referred to as cyberspace.

Today, with the Cold War an ever-dimming memory, the Internet is available to almost anyone in the world with a computer, a modem, a telephone line and an ISP. Mike Wendland estimates the worldwide Internet population is between 20 and 56 million people. The spread of his estimation is wide because the Internet is not controlled by any entity, so no one really knows how many people access it.

In 1995 Australia was said to have had the world's second-highest adoption rate of home computers, behind the United States. And in May 1997, *The Australian* reported that a Telstra consultant had estimated that by the year 2001 as many as 6.5 million Australians — a third of the 1997 total population — would be online. The same month, Edupage, an Internet newsletter of online developments, reported that Web research company Morgan Stanley had found that Australia was the third most-wired nation in the world, based on the number of networks linked to the Internet, per million population. Canada came first with 192, followed by the United States with 114 and Australia with 110. France was a distant fourth with 37, which shows how avidly Australians took to this technology. By far the most popular features of the Internet are email and the World Wide Web, and together they provide feature writers with a powerful reporting tool.

Perhaps the most defining concept of the Internet is change. Any book that seeks to describe the Internet in any detail passes into obsolescence even before it is published. And that includes this book. Consequently, the discussions here will concentrate mainly on conceptual matters rather than try to take you step by step through procedures as they exist at the time of writing but that might be gone by the time you try them. With some text-based Internet services, however, a little instruction is provided.

THE INTERNET AS A REPORTING RESOURCE

The World Wide Web and its predecessor, Gopherspace, depend on the ability of computers to talk to one another. This interactivity is possible because of a client-server connection model. A client is a program that requests information, and a server is a program that provides it. In the early days of the Internet, dumb terminals sent commands to smart computers, known as hosts. Then desktop computers took precedence. The modern version of the client-server model can be seen in its simplest form in an office where the PCs or Macs are networked to a server that holds the software programs: some of the work gets done on the desktop machine, and some on the server. The desktop computer is the client, and the server is the host.

The Internet originally was primitive compared with modern software packages and the graphics, sound and video capabilities of the World Wide Web you're probably familiar with. Even now, many universities locate their student email systems on a VAX or Unix machine, so we will discuss some text-only applications available on such machines. Because they do not load time-consuming graphics, such browsers are much faster than the modern, point-and-click versions. Because some students have text-based access, it is worth discussing these tools before moving on to the modern version of the World Wide Web with its bells and whistles.

A user logs on to a host such as a VAX or a Unix workstation and uses a complicated and non-logical text editor to produce short messages that can be transmitted in ASCII. The three basic Internet programs, according to Reddick and King, were email, Telnet and FTP. All three now can be used in a Mac or Windows point-and-click platform, but originally a user made a selection at a VAX or Unix prompt.

Using telnet and FTP

With Telnet you turn your host computer into a terminal of a remote host server. In other words, from your PC you go through your local host to obtain information from a remote host. You can access databases, commercial providers and university libraries worldwide and find specific files and information. With Telnet, you have to know the address where the file you want is held, then you Telnet to that address. Telnet keeps you advised on progress and tells you whether or not you've achieved a connection. You may see a login prompt, but the source of the address should also provide you with the login and password. When you've retrieved the desired file, you exit.

If this sounds complicated, it really isn't. In 1995, when I was on a study leave to the United States, I was able to Telnet back to QUT from borrowed local university guest accounts or from my own CompuServe account. At the prompt I would type:

>telnet qut.edu.au

Then, when I was connected to the QUT host server, it would prompt me for my QUT username and password. Typing them in, I could then operate my email account as if I were in my office at QUT or at home in my Brisbane suburb.

FTP stands for File Transfer Protocol, which is how computers communicate with one another. FTP lets you copy any file from a remote Internet host to your local host. Again, you must know the address of the remote host and what you're looking for. Your host makes the connection with the remote host. FTP accommodates people who do not have an account on the remote host machine. It allows such people to access public archives through a special account — with "anonymous" as the username and your full email address as the password.

Public archives are held in directories and subdirectories. Since you know the location of the file you want, you can move up or down this structure until you find it. FTP recognises two kinds of files: text-only, such as ASCII or DOS, and binary files containing text and formatting, such as WordPerfect or MSWord files.

Exploring gopherspace

Gopher was the first Internet browser used to locate and retrieve information from hierarchical menus. More than 2,000 Gopher servers were scattered all over the Internet. They sat waiting for requests from clients. When you reach a Gophersite, you'll find a menu that could be several screens long. Clicking on an item moves you to another menu that might be on another server on the other side of the world. And so on and so on. You could spend hours browsing the Internet, moving from menu to menu, moving from Australia to Europe to Asia to North America, pausing to download, print or email a file to yourself; to search a full-text database or to add an interesting site to your own set of bookmarks so you could go straight to it next time and not have to remember the 30 or 50 or 100 menus you traversed to find it.

Shortly after I was introduced to Gopher, I constructed a QUT Journalism Gophersite for our students to research stories or academic papers. I first bookmarked the menu items, then put them on the Gophersite. Gopher lists bookmarks in the order you collect them, but a Gophersite is in alphabetical order. Many organisations are shutting down their Gopher sites in favor of more glitzy World Wide Web pages. The QUT Journalism Gopher (No. 27 below) is gone now, but my personal bookmarks are below. Entries ending <?> are full-text databases searchable by keyword that you enter when prompted to do so. Entries ending in / are directories that may contain other directories or files. And entries with no character at the end are files.

Bookmarks

1. Journalism Resources on the Internet
2. Listservs in Journalism
3. Literature and Journalism Shelf/
4. The Journalism List
5. Journalism Periodicals Database <?>
6. Media Articles Database <?>
7. CIA World Factbook (search by word) <?>
8. Search journalism periodicals <?>
9. Vanderbilt Television News Archive/
10. Index to Communications, Journalism & English Graduate Programs
11. News and Journalism/
12. Chronicle of Higher Education/
13. The Electronic Newsstand(™)[Large collection of new journals]/
14. Campus Newspapers/
15. Daily Summaries from the White House/
16. Newspapers, Magazines, and Newsletters/
17. Virtual Reference Desk/
18. Search Gopherspace using Veronica/

---

19. Australian Weather Forecasts/
20. Other Australian Services/
21. Gopher Central Server (University Of Minnesota, USA)/
22. Other Gopher and Information Servers/
23. QUT Library Catalogue <TEL>
24. Other libraries/
25. Communications Research Centre, Ottawa, CANADA/
26. Communications Research Group, Nottingham University, (UK)/
27. Journalism Section Gopher Area/
28. Radio Free Europe/Liberty Daily News, Central & Eastern Europe/
29. Other Gopher and Information Servers/
30. Internet file server (ftp) sites/
31. Libraries/
32. News/
33. Internet Computer Index (ICI)/
34. Home Gopher server: gopher.qut.edu.au/

Gopherspace can be searched with Archie for public FTP archives and with Veronica for Gopher servers containing specific information.

Archie connects with all the FTP sites it knows about and lists all the files that are available through FTP. If your home Gopher Menu has an Archie sites item, simply select it to use it. If not, to find an Archie site, at the login prompt type archie <enter> and at the password prompt type <enter>. This will take you to Archie's opening screen and its prompt. At this prompt type set search sub <enter>, which allows you to search for partial words. At the next prompt type mail to <your email address> <enter>, which is where Archie will send your search results. These settings are good for a whole single Archie session, and have to be reset each time you use Archie. Essentially, an Archie search is a search for a computer that holds the file you want, so you have to know at least part of the filename.

When you launch Archie, it tells you your place in line and estimates how long it will take to conduct your search. Then it searches its names database. When it displays the results of your search, it shows you a list of files and their addresses. At the first prompt, type mail <enter>, and Archie will email the results to you. Exit Archie by typing quit <enter>. Then you can separately retrieve the file through normal ftp procedures.

Whereas Archie's database is made up of file names, Veronica's is made up of Gopher menu items. Most home Gopher menus have an item called Search

Gopherspace Using Veronica. After you select it, you pick a Gophersite to search. Veronica will prompt you for searchwords. Word order does not matter, partial words are acceptable, and the process is case-insensitive. Veronica's report on the results of your search comes to you in the form of a one-off Gopher menu, complete with links, based on your searchwords. You can explore this one-off menu like any other Gopher menu, but when you end your session on the host, that menu disappears from your computer.

THE WORLD WIDE WEB

The World Wide Web began as an alternative to Gopher to browse the Internet. The major difference was that Gopher used menus and the WWW used text. At a WWW text-only site you select the items you want to view, then jump to where it is held. Like Gopher, the WWW was, and is, based on the client-server model. At a WWW site, a page of straight text contains highlighted items that are actually pointers — links — to the document you want. That document could be on the same server or on any other WWW server in the world.

The text-only WWW client is known as Lynx. When you use Lynx on a WWW text-only page, the Up and Down arrows will move you from highlighted text to highlighted text. To view a highlighted item, press the Right Arrow key. The Left Arrow takes you back. Pressing the space bar takes you to the next page of text. Lynx is still available and is much faster than the point-and-click WWW browsers that have overshadowed it.

When technological advances made it possible for website servers to add graphics, photographs and video and audio clips to the text offerings, a new kind of point-and-click browser was developed to find and download these items. The major browsers are Netscape, Mosaic and Internet Explorer, and you may have used one or more of them from school, university, library or home.

These browsers follow links through the hypertext transfer protocol (http). If you think of writing on paper as two-dimensional, across the page and down the page, hypertext adds a third dimension by allowing you to write *through* the page to another page, and this other page can be on a server on the other side of the world. Around the world, thousands of government agencies, political parties, newspapers, television networks, individual television shows, lobby groups, fan clubs, freelance journalists, business writers, commercial enterprises, professional organisations and ordinary citizens have built websites from which to offer information, goods and services — some for free and some for purchase through credit card transactions.

At first glance, the Internet seems daunting, what with thousands of sites offering millions of items of information. Fortunately, navigating cyberspace to find information on specific topics has been simplified by online directories and by software programs known as search engines. These search engines treat the Internet as one giant database that you can search with keywords. Some search engines support Boolean searches and can deliver more than 10,000 "hits" in about half a minute. All browsers have built-in search engines. You'll find others just browsing homepages, especially those maintained by universities, and friends and colleagues will alert you to even more of them.

Some of the major search engines are Alta Vista, Excite, Excite Guide, HotBot, InfoSeek, Lycos, Lycos A2Z, Open Text, Webcrawler, WhatUSeek, World Wide Web Worm, WWW Yellow Pages and Yahoo. Two major search sites are Patrick's Megasearch and Dogpile. Each of those sites offers simultaneous Boolean exploration of *all* the major search engines *plus* the Usenet search engines Alta Vista News, Dejanews, Dejanews Old, Excite News, HotBot News, InfoSeek News and Reference.com, *plus* FTP search engines Filez, FTP Search and Snoopie.

On a homepage, you can explore what it has to offer just by pointing and clicking on promising topics. For example, if you were looking for a story idea, you could go to the Queensland Government Homepage where you'd find hypertext links to General Information, Queensland Government Departments and Agencies, Queensland Government Directory, Interesting Queensland Links, Other Australian governments, What's new? and Search the Site. If you click on Interesting Queensland links, you'll find hypertext links to Queensland Web, Queensland Winter Racing Carnival, Brisbane City Life, Brisbane Online, Education Resources, Global Info Links, Queensland Courts, Sunzine, Traveling Australia — Queensland, Visit Queensland, Far North Queensland Almanac, Council of the Ageing Queensland Inc., and Weather. Clicking on any of those hypertext links would take you to more information, not all of it provided by the Queensland Government. More than likely a little time spent browsing would spark an idea for a feature story.

As pointed out earlier in this chapter, universities are providing the leadership in moving Australian journalism into online reporting. For example, QUT journalism lecturer Suellen Tapsall has set up a website to aid in the teaching of a CAR unit done by all her journalism first-year students. Among the Australian links are the homepages of the Queensland and Australian Governments, the Liberal, Labor,

National Australian Democrats parties, and the Australian Consumers' Association. Among the national and international media links are the ABC, the Sydney Morning Herald, the Age, the Financial Review, AAP, New York Times, Indonesia News Network, CNN International. And among those sites she calls Interesting, Tapsall has links to the UK Police & Forensic Web, Amnesty International, United Nations, Greenpeace, Background to Arabic Nations and Information, Intelligence Links, Microsoft Corporation and Coca Cola.

Tapsall's website is an example of a resource created for journalists. There are many other such resources, some at other universities around the world and some set up by other kinds of organisations. One of the most useful among the latter is ProfNet, a resource for finding experts to add context to your stories. You can find leads on deadline, expand your contact book, explore trends. ProfNet claims to be able to help journalists on virtually any subject.

ProfNet is a collaborative of 4,000 public information officers linked by the Internet to give journalists convenient access to expert sources. ProfNet's member institutions include mostly universities, but also think tanks, national laboratories, scientific and professional associations, trade associations, medical centres, nonprofit organizations, government agencies, corporations and public relations agencies.

ProfNet is free. A journalist may conduct as many searches as he or she likes by telephone, fax or email. You can "cloak" your request so that competitors cannot steal your story. Replies go out to subscribers three times a day. ProfNet says it can routinely generate leads within two or three hours. Later in this chapter you'll see how some working journalists use the Internet for getting story ideas and researching stories, but before we get to that, you need to know a little more about email.

USING EMAIL TO DEFEAT DISTANCE AND TIME ZONES

Email allows people in far-flung corners of the globe to make and maintain personal contact. All ISPs provide their customers with an email service, and people use email more than any other Internet facility. As Reddick and King observe, email on the Internet can be used for three purposes: by one person to send a message to another person, by one person to send a message simultaneously to many other people, and by one person to post messages that are not sent directly to people's email addresses but are posted in a cyberspace location where subscribers can read them. Software packages for email range from complicated VAX/VMS systems most universities make available for their students in computer labs to sophisticated, individualised, user-friendly point-and-click systems offered by commercial ISPs and by some universities to their staff and to students for use on their home computers.

Although some email systems are more user-friendly than others, they all work the same way. When you log on, you can download the messages held by your ISP's server since your last visit. And you can compose messages. When you give the command to send it, your message zooms on the Internet across the globe, reaching its destination at best in a few minutes and at worst in a few hours at little or no cost to you. So email is much faster and less expensive than Australia Post's "snail" mail. Obviously, email is ideal for all journalists, but especially for feature writers.

Bruce Tober, an American expatriate who lives and works in the United Kingdom, told a virtual community made up mainly of journalists that he has interviewed people all around the world by email. He said it was quicker and "cheaper than phoning or traveling to Russia, Japan, Canada, Scandinavia, the US and now Australia, to do interviews" for feature stories.

Visiting virtual communities

People are social animals; since prehistoric times we have gathered into communities and sub-communities. Originally, we gathered around the watering hole and in caves for mutual support. As modern society developed, the concept of gathering together for mutual support has survived but the venues have become more sophisticated and complex. Now we gather in places like nightclubs, coffee shops, hotels, pubs, leagues clubs, bowls clubs, theatres, libraries, stadiums, cricket grounds, cinemas, RSL clubs, universities, concert halls, exercise gyms and tuck shops. In other words, after all these centuries, we still seek out and associate with other people who share our interests. So it was only natural that people with computers and modems would create virtual communities in cyberspace.

People who share an interest create virtual communities made up of individuals who live all over the world. It doesn't matter what the shared interest is — raising emus, lecturing in journalism, following the Spice Girls, collecting stamps, combating the glass ceiling, seeking cybersex, cooking Thai — there are discussion groups dedicated to it on the Internet. And they're easy to find and join.

The two most popular clusters of virtual communities are the more than 17,000 mailing lists and the nearly 72,000 Usenet newsgroups on the Internet. A mailing list is made up of people who exchange email about a subject of mutual interest. A newsgroup is similar in that it is a discussion group based on email, but rather than send messages directly to one another, its members post messages on a virtual noticeboard that others can access in their own time. Both lists can be searched by area and keyword at the Liszt WWW homepage, which you can find with a search engine.

In addition to a global search of all 72,000 mailing lists, Liszt also classifies 1,419 of the lists into 15 searchable categories — Arts, Business, Computers, Culture, Education, Health, Humanities, Music, Nature, News, Politics, Recreation, Religion, Science and Social. The 135 lists classified in Arts is further broken down into 17 sub-categories, containing one to 51 lists. Among the 15 lists in the sub-sub-category of Movies are Cinema-L, for discussion on all forms of cinema, and CJMovies, which provides film reviews and original essays on the intersection of popular culture with criminal justice, and Scrnwrit, which discusses screenwriting.

The more than 17,000 Usenet newsgroups on the Internet are broken down into nine categories — alt(ernative), biz(business), comp(uters), misc(ellaneous), news, rec(reational), sci(ence), soc(ial issues), talk. In the Australian (aus) hierarchy, there are 110 newsgroups, including such topics as ads, aviation, bushwalking, cars, films, invest, legal, motorcycles, personals, pets, politics, religion, sex, snow, theatre.

Subscribing to a mailing list is free. As a subscriber, you receive all messages sent to the list and can send messages to everyone on the list. Some lists carry heavy volume, so if you oversubscribe, you could find yourself wading through 100 or more messages each day. To ease the burden, you can get some lists in digest form: instead of receiving messages one at a time, they all come in one big package per day. There are two kinds of lists — moderated and unmoderated. On a moderated list all the messages go first to a person who screens and selects them for relay to list members. On an unmoderated list, all messages go to a computer that automatically relays them to list members.

Journalists tend to join professional and special-interest mailing lists. On professional lists they discuss with other journalists and interested non-journalists such concerns as story ideas and ethics and give and receive support, advice and camaraderie. And on special-interest lists they research specific stories. By joining a discussion list on, say, air safety or the plight of the white rhino or growing roses, journalists can quickly come up to date with current issues, problems and controversies and determine who the influential listmembers are, then contact these people privately by email. Such a list will not provide all the sources for a story, of course, but may provide insights the journalists might not have picked up with traditional reporting techniques. Finding special-interest groups is easy through Liszt. You name it and you can be certain a virtual community of individuals from around the world has formed to talk about it.

There are many professional journalism lists. Some of the major ones are CARR-L, practitioners, academics and students interested in computer-assisted reporting; IRE-L, Investigative Reporters and Editors; NICAR-L, National Institute of Computer-assisted Reporting; STUMEDIA, university journalism students; JOURNET-L, university lecturers; SPJ-L, ethics and practices. These are all listservs, which means that they automatically relay messages sent to them to all members of the list. To subscribe you send a command to the computer, which adds you to the list and sends you a welcome message with instructions for later use. The listserv address handles only automatic commands, so your typing must be letter-perfect. Messages are sent to a different address. Some relevant professional newsgroups in the alt hierarchy are alt.journalism; alt.journalism.criticism; alt.journalism.freelance; alt.journalism.gay-press; alt.journalism.students; alt.journalism.gonzo and alt.journalism.music. You can find other journalism mailing lists and newsgroups by searching Liszt. Among its hundreds of discussion groups CompuServe has a dozen or so in its Journalism Forum where professionals, students and "wannabes" exchange information in such areas as freelancing, investigative reporting, covering music, the news business itself.

When you join a listserv or a newsgroup, you usually receive its list of Frequently Asked Questions (FAQs). List members learned early on that as "newbies" joined their list, they tended to ask the same questions as previous newbies. The questions tended to be the obvious ones that anyone new would ask. So take the time to read the FAQs before you jump in. As well, it's a good idea to "lurk" for a while before joining a discussion or asking questions. Some of the professionals on CARR-L, for example, want to restrict discussions to comparisons of hardware and software and resent students asking for help in doing assignments. Over on JOURNET-L, by contrast, which is populated by many lecturers, such student requests are warmly received. Lurking gives you a chance to get the feel of the list, what kinds of topics are welcomed and disparaged. As well, you can figure out who the opinion leaders are.

Because the Internet is a loose anarchy, its success depends on its users following certain conventions — Netiquette — aimed at keeping discussions friendly. Chief among the rules of the road are respect and tolerance for the opinions of others. Occasionally debates can turn nasty when one participant "flames" another. A flame is a personal attack, and these can be vicious. Since your aim is to elicit information from your listmates, you have a vested interest in being polite to everyone you encounter in cyberspace, even the nasties.

Do not assume that email is private. Employers, ISPs and universities have been known to "eavesdrop" on people using their email and browsing systems. So your activities can be tracked, because computers retain copies of everything. This means that if the topic is confidential or you must protect a source, don't commit much to email.

JOURNALISTS DISCUSS ONLINE REPORTING

Once a feature writer has an idea, it's a good idea use a search engine to see what's on the WWW. Freelancer Ruth Carapella says that she does an advanced query search in Alta Vista. For one article, she did a Boolean search on "areotriangulation and GPS" and found links to 15 documents, including symposium proceedings that were very useful. This information enabled her to draft a set of interview questions.

Elizabeth Walton found that as a freelance feature writer living in rural New South Wales, gathering information for a report on Sydney's Green Olympics was difficult, because many of the reports she needed were from overseas sources. Using the Internet, she gathered all the background information she required, including details of Atlanta's achievements for the 1996 Games and a summary of the Rio Earth Summit's Agenda 21 — the document which lead to the "greening up" of the Olympics. The background was important because she had to explain to readers why the Olympics had got on the "green" bandwagon.

She began by searching the WWW for any sites matching the "Olympics" keyword. "This brought me to the Team Energy Atlanta home page, where I found all the material I needed to begin a comparative analysis between environmental standards in the 1996 Olympics and Sydney's 2000 Olympics," she wrote. "I also visited the Sydney2000 site, and downloaded Sydney's Environmental Guidelines — a key document in the story — and found an Olympics Telnet site, which is a virtual library of past Olympics stories." She also found Atlanta sources available by email.

Walton cited another advantage of online research: because you conduct the research at your desk you save time and because time is money, you also save money. "Spending time driving to a resource centre, finding your information and then driving home again seems to be a waste of time," she said. "Much better to dial up, use a browser to locate the info, send a few emails to potential sources, and then move on to the writing phase."

Many online journalists use a combination of email and online searches in their work. Freelance feature writer Sophia Dembling estimates that she divides her online time 70 per cent email and 30 per cent other usages, primarily searching the WWW. "I use the Web to track down good sources, use email to make initial contact, then interview them on the telephone," she wrote. She uses the Web to find sources all over the US, relieving her from reliance on only local sources.

Kimberley Ivory, a freelance feature writer who lives in rural New South Wales, uses a similar method to overcome the tyranny of distance. To put a human face on a story on traveling with babies for *Open Road*, Ivory wanted to interview people who had done it. She asked a discussion group for help, got a few responses and followed the leads up with lists of questions by email. For another story on pregnancy, she collected anecdotes by electronically posting messages in appropriate discussion groups asking for women's best pregnancy advice. She received 30 replies, plenty for the story.

At the time we corresponded by email, Ivory was doing an investigative piece for which she wanted to interview a testy Harvard professor who had recently visited Australia. To track him down in the United States, she had posted a note in one of CompuServe's Journalism forums and within 24 hours had obtained the professor's email address. She wrote and asked if he'd be willing to be interviewed by email. He agreed and gave her some great quotes and useful background material. On his Australian visit, the professor had been prickly and uncooperative with the press. "He was very forthright and open, which is something else which happens on email, I think," Ivory wrote. She found email particularly convenient, as her overseas source was many time zones away. Under such circumstances, the questions can flow at the convenience of the writer, and the answers at the convenience of the source.

Naturally, email is not going to supplant such traditional tools as the telephone any time soon. Jo Oliphant of the *Courier-Mail* is fairly typical with her observation that the telephone "is more personal and many people still don't have e-mail access". So she conducts most of her interviews by telephone. But on one occasion she found that email won her interviews that she had failed to get by telephone. She was doing an article on lobby groups that bypass the news media and use websites to disseminate information. At the height of the national debate over the Northern Territory's euthanasia legislation she was able to interview by email Des Carne, the creator of the Deliverance Euthanasia site, and Philip Nitschke, the Northern Territory pro-euthanasia doctor. "Mr Carne was a little wary of the media and was keen to provide written responses to my questions," Oliphant wrote. "As for Mr Nitschke, he was simply too busy to speak to me on the phone, but spared a few minutes late one night to send me an email."

Marsha Woodbury, Director of Information Technology at the University of Illinois' Graduate School of Library and Information Science, speaks highly in favor of the email interview for feature stories and is well aware of its pitfalls. She points out that the source can keep a copy of the answers, that there is time for the source to consider his or her responses, that the interview can be conducted without taking time for an appointment, and that the chance of misquoting the source is minimal, especially if you cut-and-paste from your email software to your word processor. She says there are three main disadvantages to email: you can't view body language or ask quick follow-up questions, and "if you are involved in an intricate investigative reporting venture, this method is going to allow people time to run for cover".

These are not the only disadvantages. In a discussion on the CompuServe JForum freelance list, a writer said that her editor was concerned that the people she interviewed by email for a story on Attention Deficit Disorder might not be who they said they were. The editor wanted her to confirm by telephone that there really was a Joe Bloggs who had ADD, that it was not someone having her on. Several listmates responded that the editor's request was legitimate. Most agreed that a telephone follow-up was appropriate.

Writer James K. Kling was one of them. He wrote that if you're unsure about an on-line interview — or if you feel it is incomplete — do a follow-up phone interview. He said he does this routinely. He gets the information through email, then looks over the answers and digests them. Then he conducts a short telephone interview, finding that because he is better informed, he can ask more pointed questions.

Of course normal precautions must be taken, as with any source. But on the telephone you also have to make sure that the person on the other end of the line is Joe Bloggs, not someone who's having you on. Yet because telephones have been around longer than email, when we ask, "Joe Bloggs, with ADD?" and the voice answers yes, we assume it is indeed Joe Bloggs. Why? And how is the situation different with email? If you take the normal precautions, you should have confidence in the identity of the people you interview by email.

There is a convenience factor in interviewing by email. Freelancer Peggy Noonan, who routinely emails lists of questions to interviewees, notes that it's obviously convenient for the source. But, she says, it's also convenient for her because she can copy and paste the email content straight into her story — as I did in writing this chapter, by the way.

In fact, I used basic CAR techniques to conduct virtually all the research for this chapter as a demonstration of their utility. Web browsing, listserv lurking and email interviewing came into the research everywhere except for some definitions, explanations and examples found in books; journal articles by Green, by Johnson, by Tapsall, by Quinn and by Woodbury and Schmitz; the Charlton paragraph on the McLachlan appointment, which I clipped from the *Courier-Mail*; and Mike Wendland's database entry advice, which I heard at the Poynter Institute in 1995.

Knowing that eventually I would write this chapter, for the last couple of years I had subscribed to several professional listservs on which CAR was a frequent topic of discussion. I kept personal email interviews and discussion list postings in a dedicated mailbox in my email software package, Eudora Pro 3.0. Then I imported the whole mailbox into askSam, a free-form, full-text database that supports Boolean searches. Locating the cogent quotations by using keywords, I cut and pasted them into the text of the chapter and with a little fiddling made them fit into my sentences. The result, I hope, encourages you in your own efforts to produce better feature stories through computer-assisted reporting.

SOURCES AND SUGGESTIONS FOR FURTHER READING

Berner, R.T. (1988). *Writing literary features*. Hillsdale, N.J.: Lawrence Erlbaum Associates, Publishers. An excellent source for writers seeking to learn the advanced techniques of creative nonfiction, also called literary journalism.

Franklin, J. (1986). *Writing for story: craft secrets of dramatic nonfiction by a two-time Pulitzer Prize winner*. New York: Plume. An excellent source for writers seeking to learn the advanced techniques of creative nonfiction, also called literary journalism.

Green, K. (1994). "Computer-assisted reporting — sources from cyberspace", *Australian Studies in Journalism*, 3:219–230. Green's change of heart was reported by Quinn.

Houston, B. (1996). *Computer-assisted reporting: a practical guide*. New York: St Martin's Press.

Johnson, J.T. (1994). "Applied cybernetics and its implications for education for journalism", *Australian Journalism Review*, 16(2):55–66.

Lorenz, A.L., and Vivian, J. (1996). *News: reporting and writing*. Boston: Allyn & Bacon.

Paul, N. (1995). *Computer assisted research: a guide to tapping online information*, 3rd ed. St Petersburg, Fla.: Poynter Institute for Media Studies. Also available on the Poynter website: http://www.poynter.org

Quinn, S. (1997). "Computer-assisted reporting in Australia", *Australian Journalism Review*, 19(1):77–90.

Reddick, R. and King, E. (1997). *The online journalist: using the Internet and other electronic resources*, 2nd ed. Fort Worth: Harcourt Brace College Publishers.

Tapsall, S. (1997). "Can Australian journalists drive the US CAR?" *Australian Journalism Review*, 19(1):69–76.

Wendland, M. (1996). *Wired journalist: newsroom guide to the Internet*. n.c.: Radio and Television News Directors Foundation.

Woodbury, M., and Schmitz, J. (1994). "Ethics the driver, Mosaic the vehicle, network instruction the cargo", *Australian Journalism Review*, 16(1): 94–98.

INDEX